6.10

PUBLISHERS' NOTE

The series in which this title appears was introduced by the publishers in 1957 and is under the general editorship of Dr. Maurice G. Kendall. It is intended to fill a need which has been evident for some time and is likely to grow—the need for some form of publication at moderate cost which will make accessible to a group of readers specialized studies in statistics or special courses on particular statistical topics. There are numerous cases where, for example, a monograph on some newly developed field would be very useful, but the subject has not reached the stage where a comprehensive book is possible or, again, where a course of study is desired in a domain not covered by textbooks but where an exhaustive treatment, even if possible, would be expensive and perhaps too elaborate for the readers' needs.

Considerable attention has been given to the problem of producing these books speedily and economically. Appearing in a cover the design of which will be standard, the contents of each volume will follow a simple, straightforward layout, the text production method adopted being suited to the complexity or otherwise of the subject.

The publishers will be interested in approaches from any authors who have work of importance suitable for the series.

CHARLES GRIFFIN & CO. LTD.

OTHER BOOKS ON MATHEMATICS AND STATISTICS

Games, gods and gambling	F. N. DAVID
Combinatorial chance	F. N. DAVID and D. E. BARTON
A statistical primer	F. N. DAVID
An introduction to the theory of statistics	G. U. YULE and M. G. KENDALL
The advanced theory of statistics (three volumes)	M. G. KENDALL and A. STUART
Rank correlation methods	M. G. KENDALL
Exercises in theoretical statistics	M. G. KENDALL
Rapid statistical calculations	M. H. QUENOUILLE
The design and analysis of experiment	M. H. QUENOUILLE
Sampling methods for censuses and surveys	F. YATES
Biomathematics	C. A. B. SMITH
Statistical method in biological assay	D. J. FINNEY
The mathematical theory of epidemics	N. T. J. BAILEY
Probability and the weighing of evidence	I. J. GOOD

GRIFFIN'S STATISTICAL MONOGRAPHS AND COURSES:

No. 1: *The analysis of multiple time-series*	M. H. QUENOUILLE
No. 2: *A course in multivariate analysis*	M. G. KENDALL
No. 3: *The fundamentals of statistical reasoning*	M. H. QUENOUILLE
No. 4: *Basic ideas of scientific sampling*	A. STUART
No. 5: *Characteristic functions*	E. LUKACS
No. 6: *An introduction to infinitely many variates*	E. A. ROBINSON
No. 7: *Mathematical methods in the theory of queueing*	A. Y. KHINTCHINE
No. 8: *A course in the geometry of* n *dimensions*	M. G. KENDALL
No. 9: *Random wavelets and cybernetic systems*	E. A. ROBINSON
No. 10: *Geometrical probability*	M. G. KENDALL and P. A. P. MORAN
No. 11: *An introduction to symbolic programming*	P. WEGNER
No. 12: *The method of paired comparisons*	H. A. DAVID

Descriptive leaflets available from Charles Griffin & Co. Ltd.

GEOMETRICAL PROBABILITY

M. G. KENDALL, M.A., Sc.D.

Formerly Professor of Statistics in the University of London
President of the Royal Statistical Society 1960–62

and

P. A. P. MORAN, M.A., D.Sc.

Professor of Statistics in the Australian National University

BEING NUMBER TEN OF
GRIFFIN'S STATISTICAL
MONOGRAPHS & COURSES

EDITED BY

M. G. KENDALL, M.A., Sc.D.

CHARLES GRIFFIN & COMPANY LIMITED
LONDON

First published in 1963

Printed in Great Britain by Butler & Tanner Ltd, Frome and London

PREFACE

To the best of our knowledge, no book on this subject has been published since Deltheil's excellent little brochure *Probabilités géométriques* of 1926. Not only does no book exist in English, but most textbooks on probability completely ignore applications in the geometrical field. The reason, we suppose, is that by 1900 the set of beautiful results obtained by Morgan Crofton and others seemed to have exhausted the subject.

In the last twenty years a large number of problems have arisen which require for their solution all that was discovered in the past about geometrical probabilities and a great deal more besides. The subject, in fact, has been reborn. A glance through the examples in this book will illustrate the breadth of the field of current application: astronomy, atomic physics, biology, crystallography, petrography, sampling theory, sylviculture—all contribute, to say nothing of sundry classified subjects which we were not free to mention.

We hope, therefore, that this book, in bringing together the theory of the subject, in describing some of the applications, and in raising some of the unsolved problems, will serve a useful purpose to scientists of all kinds. We also hope that it will bring to the attention of mathematicians a subject of great intellectual charm with many challenging fields for further research.

M. G. K.
P. A. P. M.

London, England
Canberra, Australia
June, 1962

CONTENTS

8

CHAPTER 1

DISTRIBUTIONS OF GEOMETRICAL ELEMENTS

The probability measure of geometrical elements

1.1 In probability theory one is usually concerned with random variables which are quantities, or sets of quantities, taking values in some set of possibilities on which there is defined a non-negative measure, satisfying certain required conditions which enable us to interpret it as a probability. In the theory of geometrical probabilities the random elements are not quantities but geometrical objects such as points, lines and rotations. Since the ascription of a measure to such elements is not quite an obvious procedure, a number of "paradoxes" can be produced by failure to distinguish the reference set. These are all based on a simple confusion of ideas but may be useful in illustrating the way in which geometric probabilities should be defined.

1.2 We consider one due to J. Bertrand (1907). The problem is to find the probability that a "random chord" of a circle of unit radius has a length greater than $\sqrt{3}$, the side of an inscribed equilateral triangle. We may consider three possible solutions of this problem.

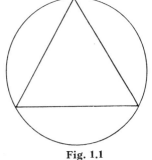

(1) Any chord of the circle intersects it in two points, and we may suppose these to be independently distributed in probability distributions which are uniform over the circumference of the circle. Without loss of generality we can suppose one of the two points to be at a vertex of an inscribed equilateral triangle. There is then just $\frac{1}{3}$ of the circumference in which the other point can lie in order that the resulting chord has

Fig. 1.1

length greater than $\sqrt{3}$, so that the probability is $\frac{1}{3}$.

(2) The length of the chord depends on its distance from the centre of the circle and not on its direction. We may therefore suppose that it has a fixed direction perpendicular to a given diameter of the circle and that its point of intersection with this diameter has a uniform distribution. For the chord to have a length greater than $\sqrt{3}$ the distance of the point of intersection from the centre of the circle must be less than $\frac{1}{2}$, so that the probability is $\frac{1}{2}$.

(3) Any chord is uniquely defined by the foot of a perpendicular on it from the centre. If this point is distributed uniformly over the circle the probability of it lying in any region of area A is $A\pi^{-1}$ since the total area of the circle is π. For the chord to have length greater than $\sqrt{3}$ the foot of the perpendicular must lie inside a circle of radius $\frac{1}{2}$ and hence the probability is $\frac{1}{4}$.

1.3 All three solutions are correct, but they really refer to different problems. In all questions concerning geometrical probability we have first to define what is meant by the phrase "at random". If we consider the chord as being determined by the angle θ which it makes with a fixed direction, and by its distance p from the centre of the circle, the determination of what is meant by "at random" is equivalent to determining a joint probability density for θ and p on their range of variation which is $(0 \leqslant \theta < 2\pi, 0 \leqslant p \leqslant 1)$. In the first solution of Bertrand's example let α and β be the angular coordinates of the ends of the chord, so that $0 \leqslant \alpha, \beta \leqslant 2\pi$ and the joint probability distribution is $(2\pi)^{-2} d\alpha\, d\beta$. We also have

$$\alpha, \beta = \theta \pm \cos^{-1} p$$

so that by changing variables we see that the joint probability distribution of θ and p must be given by

$$\frac{dp\, d\theta}{2\pi \sqrt{(1-p^2)}}.$$

Similarly in the second solution the distribution of p and θ is given by

$$(2\pi)^{-1} dp\, d\theta,$$

and in the third by

$$(\pi)^{-1} p\, dp\, d\theta.$$

1.4 In general, to define the distribution of a geometric object we must first determine a system of coordinates which define the object uniquely, and then define a probability distribution on the range of these coordinates. As examples of such coordinates we may consider the following:—

(1) Points in Euclidean space of one, two, three, or more dimensions can be defined by their Cartesian coordinates. Here the parameter space coincides with the space of elements.

(2) Lines in two-dimensional space may be defined by their intersection with one of the axes and the angle they make with this axis, or by the latter and their shortest distance from the origin. Similarly, lines in three dimensions can be defined by the coordinates of their intersec-

tion with a given plane, and their direction. They therefore require four coordinates for their complete specification. We could also define a straight line by its six Plücker coordinates, but this is no longer a unique representation since the line depends only on the ratios of these coordinates, and in addition there is an equation connecting them. This makes the setting up of a probability measure in the corresponding case more difficult, and it is nearly always desirable to represent a geometric object in a coordinate space in such a way that, not only is there a one-to-one correspondence, but the set in the space corresponding to all possible objects has the same dimensionality as the coordinate space.

(3) A plane in three dimensions can be determined by the coefficients (u, v, w) of its representation as a linear equation in Cartesian coordinates,

$$ux + vy + wz + 1 = 0,$$

or, what is often much more convenient, by its distance p from the origin, and the polar co-ordinates θ, ϕ of the perpendicular from the origin on to the plane. In any case the coordinate space must be three-dimensional.

(4) A translation in three dimensions may be represented by the three coordinates, (a, b, c) say, of the point which is taken as the new origin of coordinates.

(5) A rotation in three dimensions may also be represented by three coordinates. These could be taken as the polar coordinates θ, ϕ of the axis of rotation, together with the angle, ψ, of rotation. Alternatively, since any rotation in three dimensions can be represented by an orthogonal matrix, we could take any three elements of this matrix which are independent, since such a matrix is determined by any three such elements.

1.5 We notice that in all the above examples, with the exception of rotation, the set of possible coordinates has an infinite measure or volume. On the other hand, if we place further restrictions on the geometrical objects we may obtain sets in the coordinate space which are bounded. Thus, for example, the coordinates corresponding to all planes in three dimensions which intersect a bounded figure themselves form a bounded set.

1.6 If we have a fixed number of geometric elements we may define their joint probability distribution in the space of the coordinates. Suppose that the coordinates defining the element are $(z_1 ..., z_k)$ in a space Ω which may or may not be bounded. Representing the coordinates by a vector $\mathbf{z}$, we suppose that we have a non-negative measure $P(E)$, defined on an additive class of sets E in the space Ω, which is such that

$$P(\Omega) = \int_{\Omega} dP = 1.$$

In most cases, $P(E)$ will be the Lebesgue integral of a continuous or fairly regular function over the sets E, and the additive class can be taken as all those sets which are measurable in the Lebesgue sense.

1.7 The probability distribution of a fixed number of geometric elements which are independent can then be taken as the product of such distributions. However, we also need to consider cases where the number of elements is itself a random variable. The most natural assumption to make is that the number of elements in any specified subset E of Ω has a Poisson distribution independently of the number in any other disjoint set, so that the number N of elements in E has probability $e^{-\lambda}\lambda^N(N!)^{-1}$, where λ depends on E. This is a consistent definition since the sum of two independent Poisson variates is itself a Poisson variate.

1.8 Hence we define a measure $M(E)$ on the space Ω of all possible parameter points. This measure will usually not be bounded, i.e. $M(\Omega)$ may be infinite, but it will be σ-finite, that is to say that Ω can be decomposed into a finite or enumerably infinite number of sets E_1, $E_2, \ldots$, such that

$$\Omega = E_1 + E_2 + \ldots$$

and $M(E_i)$ is finite for every i. Consider, for example, random points on a line and suppose that the number occurring in any interval of length 1 is a Poisson variate with mean 1, and is independent of what happens outside this interval. Then $M(E)$ will be equal to the Lebesgue measure for any Lebesgue measurable set E on the line, and although $M(\Omega)$, the length of the whole line, in infinite, Ω can be represented as the sum of an enumerable number of intervals of finite length.

1.9 Let N be the number of geometric elements whose parameters lie in the set E in the parameter space. N is a Poisson variate with mean

$$\lambda = M(E) = \int_E dM, \qquad (1.1)$$

and therefore has a generating function

$$\exp(z-1)\lambda \int_E dM. \qquad (1.2)$$

Conditional on the fact that there are exactly N such elements, the joint distribution of their coordinates $z_1, \ldots, z_N$ is

$$\frac{dM(z_1)\dots dM(z_N)}{\left\{\int_E dM(z)\right\}^N} \tag{1.3}$$

so that for $N = 1$ we get a relationship between the measure $M(E)$ and the correspondingly induced $P(E)$. When $M(E)$ is not the integral of its derivative, (1.3) can be similarly interpreted when integrated over any subset, G say, of E. Then the probability of a single element having its coordinates in G, if it is known that they are in E, is

$$p(G \mid E) = \frac{\int_{GE} dM(z)}{\int_E dM(z)}, \tag{1.4}$$

where GE is the set common to E and G. Notice that $p(G \mid E)$ is a set function of two sets E and G.

1.10 A problem in geometrical probability will, therefore, not be defined until we have chosen a probability measure $P(E)$ in the case of a fixed number of independently distributed elements, or a measure $M(E)$ in the case of a random number. Such a choice is quite arbitrary in general, and it is the failure to recognize this fact which leads to "paradoxes". However, some choices of such measures are both more useful and more intuitively sensible than others, and we need to consider some criterion of choice.

Choice of a probability measure

1.11 Most problems in geometrical probability are concerned with elements in Euclidean space and with properties which are invariant under the group of transformations which is appropriate to Euclidean space, i.e. all translations, rotations and reflections. Consider then a set A of geometric objects in Euclidean space. We obtain all translations by transforming the coordinates by addition of constants, and all rotations and reflections by transforming them by an orthogonal transformation. For example in a three-dimensional space the coordinates x, y, z will be transformed into new coordinates x', y', z' by

$$x' = x_0 + a_{11}x + a_{12}y + a_{13}z,$$
$$y' = y_0 + a_{21}x + a_{22}y + a_{23}z,$$
$$z' = z_0 + a_{31}x + a_{32}y + a_{33}z, \tag{1.5}$$

where (a_{ij}) is an orthogonal matrix and the set A will be transformed into a new set A'. If the set of parameter points corresponding to A in the parameter space is E, the set corresponding to A' will be E', a transformation of the set E induced by the transformation in the Euclidean space, and in the choice of $P(E)$ or $M(E)$ we naturally impose the condition that $P(E') = P(E)$, or $M(E') = M(E)$. Thus the choice of these measures depends on the measure-preserving properties of such groups of transformations.

As particular examples we consider in paragraphs **1.12–1.20** the following five cases.

Points in Euclidean space of n dimensions

1.12 Here the parameter space is the same as the space of elements, and if the measure of a set is to be invariant under translations and rotations, the natural measure to use is Lebesgue measure. If we are considering the distribution of a single point, or a finite number of points, we cannot allow it to range over the whole of any set with infinite measure but must confine it to a region of the space with bounded measure (e.g. the inside of a cube, or sphere). Let this region be R and its Lebesgue measure be $m(R)$. Then we take $P(E)$, the probability of the point lying within a set E contained in R, to be

$$P(E) = \frac{m(E)}{m(R)}.$$

If we are dealing with an arbitrary (i.e. random) number of points, we suppose that the number of such points lying in a set E of finite Lebesgue measure is a Poisson variate with mean $\lambda m(E) = M(E)$, where λ is a constant. If the number of such points is n, the conditional distribution that they lie in sets $E_1, ..., E_n$ contained in E, given n, is

$$\frac{m(E_1) ... m(E_n)}{m(E)^n},$$

provided they have each been provided with suffixes so that they can be distinguished.

Straight lines in two-dimensional space

1.13 Suppose these are defined by equations of the form:

$$ux + vy + 1 = 0. \tag{1.6}$$

Then u and v may be regarded as the coordinates of the line, and the parameter space is the two-dimensional space with coordinates (u, v), excluding the point $(0, 0)$. The representation excludes lines passing through the origin, but this will not cause any difficulty. A translation and rotation in the two-dimensional plane can be represented by the algebraic transformation:

$$X = a + x \cos \alpha - y \sin \alpha,$$
$$Y = b + x \sin \alpha + y \cos \alpha,$$

where a, b are arbitrary constants, and $0 \leqslant \alpha < 2\pi$. The new position of the line after the transformation will be given by

$$UX + VY + 1 = 0 \tag{1.7}$$

where

$$u = \frac{U \cos \alpha + V \sin \alpha}{aU + bV + 1}, \tag{1.8}$$

$$v = \frac{-U \sin \alpha + V \cos \alpha}{aU + bV + 1}, \tag{1.9}$$

and in the new position the line must again not pass through the origin as otherwise the denominator in (1.8) and (1.9) would vanish. Now suppose we look for a measure function, $M(E)$, defined by an integral of the form

$$\iint_E F(u, v) \, du \, dv,$$

which we want to equal

$$\iint_{E'} F(U, V) \, dU \, dV.$$

The former is equal to

$$\iint_E F(u, v) \frac{\partial(u, v)}{\partial(U, V)} \, dU \, dV$$

where

$$\frac{\partial(u, v)}{\partial(U, V)} = \begin{vmatrix} \dfrac{\partial u}{\partial U} & \dfrac{\partial u}{\partial V} \\[2ex] \dfrac{\partial v}{\partial U} & \dfrac{\partial v}{\partial V} \end{vmatrix} \tag{1.10}$$

Since equality is to hold for all sets E', we must have

$$F(U, V) = F(u, v) \frac{\partial(u, v)}{\partial(U, V)}. \tag{1.11}$$

Straightforward evaluation of the Jacobian (1.10) gives

$$\frac{\partial(u, v)}{\partial(U, V)} = (aU + bV + 1)^{-3}$$

Squaring (1.8) and (1.9) and adding, we get

$$(aU + bV + 1)^{-3} = (u^2 + v^2)^{\frac{3}{2}} (U^2 + V^2)^{-\frac{3}{2}},$$

so that (1.11) will be satisfied if we take $F(u, v)$ proportional to

$$(u^2 + v^2)^{-\frac{3}{2}},$$

and

$$M(E) = \iint_E \frac{du\,dv}{(u^2+v^2)^{\frac{3}{2}}}. \tag{1.12}$$

Notice that for this technique to work we require that the Jacobian be of the form $\phi(u, ...)\,\phi(U, ...)^{-1}$. Having found $M(E)$ we can then find $P(E)$, the probability corresponding to a single line, whenever the latter is restricted by conditions which ensure that the coordinates u and v lie outside some circle of non-zero radius surrounding the origin in the (u, v) plane. This ensures that the integral (1.12) converges.

1.14 In many applications it is more convenient to represent a line in a plane by the polar coordinates of the point where the perpendicular from the origin meets it. If these are (p, θ) we can write the equation of the line as

$$\frac{x\cos\theta}{-p} + \frac{y\sin\theta}{-p} + 1 = 0$$

and the differential element

$$\frac{du\,dv}{(u^2+v^2)^{\frac{3}{2}}}$$

transforms into

$$dp\,d\theta, \tag{1.13}$$

because we can put

$$u = -p^{-1}\cos\theta, \quad v = -p^{-1}\sin\theta,$$

so that

$$\frac{\partial(u, v)}{\partial(p, \theta)} = p^3,$$

and

$$(u^2+v^2)^{\frac{3}{2}} = p^3.$$

Notice that (1.13) corresponds to the second solution of Bertrand's problem. Moreover, (1.13) is nearly obvious as the natural measure invariant under translations, rotations and reflections. Poincaré (1912) has shown that (1.13) is the only such differential element which remains invariant under the group of all translations and rotations.

Straight lines in three-dimensional space

1.15 Such lines form a four-dimensional manifold and therefore require four parameters. It is convenient to represent them by the equations

$$x = az+p,$$
$$y = bz+q, \tag{1.14}$$

so that (a, b, p, q) are the parameters of the line in a four-dimensional space. This omits the set of all lines parallel to the plane $z = 0$, but as these will turn out to have zero measure this will cause no difficulty. We could now proceed exactly as before by considering the effect on these parameters of all translations and orthogonal transformations. However, it is of some interest to illustrate the method of finding such invariant measures by studying infinitesimal transformations in this case.

1.16 Suppose that we have a space determined by n coordinates $(x_1, ..., x_n)$ and a continuous group of transformations which is itself determined by r parameters. We look for an integral of the form

$$J = \int ... \int F(x_1, ..., x_n) dx_1 ... dx_n \tag{1.15}$$

which is to be invariant under any transformation of the group, and must therefore, in particular, be invariant under any infinitesimal transformation of the group.†

Suppose the transformations of the group can be represented as

$$x_i' = f_i(x_1, ..., x_n \, a_1, ..., a_v), \tag{1.16}$$

where $i = 1, ..., n$. Then one possible infinitesimal transformation from x to x' will be of the form

$$x_i' = x_i + \xi_i(x_1, ..., x_n) \delta t \tag{1.17}$$

where δt is an infinitesimal of the first order and the ξ_i are to be determined. The Jacobian of this transformation will be

$$\Delta = \begin{vmatrix} 1 + \dfrac{\partial \xi_1}{\partial x_1} \delta t & \dfrac{\partial \xi_1}{\partial x_2} \delta t & . & . & . \\[2ex] \dfrac{\partial \xi_2}{\partial x_1} & 1 + \dfrac{\partial \xi_2}{\partial x_2} \delta t & . & . & . \\[2ex] . & . & . & . & . \\[2ex] . & . & . & . & 1 + \dfrac{\partial \xi_n}{\partial x_n} \delta t \end{vmatrix}$$

$$= 1 + \left(\frac{\partial \xi_1}{\partial x_1} + ... + \frac{\partial \xi_n}{\partial x_n} \right) \delta t + 0(\delta t^2).$$

The effect of the transformation on F will be to turn it into $F + \delta F$ where

$$\delta F = \sum_i \xi_i \frac{\partial F}{\partial x_i} \delta t$$

† Deltheil (1926) gives a more extended discussion of infinitesimal groups and their infinitesimal generators. See also Santaló (1953).

G.P.—B

and so J becomes

$$\int \ldots \int \{F + \delta F\}\left\{1 + \delta t \Sigma \frac{\partial \xi_i}{\partial x_i}\right\} dx_1 \ldots dx_n.$$

If J is to remain invariant under all such transformations, we must have

$$\delta F + F \delta t \Sigma \frac{\partial \xi_i}{\partial x_i} = 0. \tag{1.18}$$

Inserting the value of F we get

$$\delta t\left\{\Sigma_i \frac{\partial}{\partial x_i}(F\xi_i)\right\} = 0$$

which is to be true for all t so that

$$\Sigma_i \frac{\partial}{\partial x_i}(F\xi_i) = 0.$$

There will be r independent infinitesimal transformations corresponding to the r parameters $a_1, \ldots, a_r$ so that there are r sets of functions ξ_i which we shall denote by $(\xi_{1j} \ldots \xi_{nj})$ $(j = 1, \ldots, r)$. We therefore have r independent equations

$$\Sigma_i \frac{\partial}{\partial x_i}(F\xi_{ij}) = 0 \tag{1.19}$$

which will, in general, be sufficient to determine F.

1.17 In the case of random lines in a three-dimensional space we have four coordinates (a, b, p, q) for each line and we wish to find a function F such that

$$J = \int\int\int\int F(a, b, p, q)\, da\, db\, dp\, dq$$

is invariant under translations, rotations and reflections. The group of transformations has six parameters, and the infinitesimal transformations can be taken as infinitesimal translations in the directions of the x, y, and z axes, and infinitesimal rotations about these axes. For each of these we have to study the effect on the coefficients a, b, p, and q.

From (1.14) we see that the translation $x' = x + \delta t$ results in

$$a' = a$$

and

$$p' = p - \delta t; \tag{1.20}$$

and similarly $y' = y + \delta t$ results in

$$b' = b$$

$$q' = q - \delta t. \tag{1.21}$$

The translation $z' = z + \delta t$ has the double effect

$$a' = a, \quad p' = p + a\,\delta t,$$
$$b' = b, \quad q' = q + b\,\delta t. \tag{1.22}$$

The rotation δt around the z axis results in

$$x' = x - y\,\delta t = az + p,$$
$$y' = y + x\,\delta t = bz + q,$$

and solving as a pair of equations in x and y, and ignoring terms which are of $o(\delta t)$, we find

$$x = (a + b\,\delta t)z + p + q\,\delta t,$$
$$y = (b - a\,\delta t)z + q - p\,\delta t,$$

so that the induced transformations are

$$a' = a + b\,\delta t,$$
$$b' = b - a\,\delta t,$$
$$p' = p + q\,\delta t,$$
$$q' = q - p\,\delta t. \tag{1.23}$$

The rotation round the x axis given by

$$\delta y = -z\,\delta t, \quad \delta z = y\,\delta t$$

results in the pair of equations:

$$x = a(z + y\,\delta t) + p,$$
$$y - z\,\delta t = b(z + y\,\delta t) + q.$$

The effect of this on the parameters is therefore given by:

$$a' = a + ab\,\delta t,$$
$$b' = b + (1 + b^2)\,\delta t,$$
$$p' = p + aq\,\delta t,$$
$$q' = q + bq\,\delta t, \tag{1.24}$$

which are obtained by transforming the pairs of equations into the standard form and omitting terms of $o(\delta t)$. Similarly the rotation about the y axis gives:

$$a' = a + (1 + a^2)\,\delta t,$$
$$b' = b + ab\,\delta t,$$
$$p' = p + ap\,\delta t,$$
$$q' = q + bp\,\delta t. \tag{1.25}$$

Equations (1.20)–(1.25) give the values of ξ_{ij} in (1.18) for each of the six transformations. For example, from (1.20) and (1.17) we see that for the first transformation, of the four values of ξ corresponding to a, b, p, q in that order, three are zero and $\xi_3 = -1$. Equation (1.19) then gives

$$\frac{\partial F}{\partial p} = 0 \qquad (1.26)$$

and likewise

$$\frac{\partial F}{\partial q} = 0. \qquad (1.27)$$

(1.26) and (1.27) imply that F is independent of p and q. Equation (1.22) then leads to

$$\frac{\partial}{\partial p}(aF) + \frac{\partial}{\partial q}(bF) = 0 \qquad (1.28)$$

and this is identically true. The fourth equation becomes

$$\frac{\partial}{\partial a}(bF) - \frac{\partial}{\partial b}(aF) = b\frac{\partial F}{\partial a} - a\frac{\partial F}{\partial b} = 0. \qquad (1.29)$$

This immediately implies that F is a function of $a^2 + b^2$ only, since it does not vary when we vary a and b in any manner which keeps $a^2 + b^2$ constant. Hence we can write $F = \phi(a^2 + b^2)$, and the fifth and sixth equations are then both equivalent to

$$(1 + a^2 + b^2)\phi'(a^2 + b^2) + 2\phi(a^2 + b^2) = 0$$

so that

$$F = (1 + a^2 + b^2)^{-2}, \qquad (1.30)$$

or some multiple of this.

This implies, just as we might expect, that all points on the plane $z = 0$ are equiprobable (if restricted to any bounded region) and that all directions are equally probable.

Planes in three-dimensional space

1.18 We can determine such planes by the length of the perpendiculars on them from the origin together with the polar coordinates of these perpendiculars, so that their equations in Cartesian coordinates are

$$x \sin\theta \cos\phi + y \sin\theta \sin\phi + z \cos\theta = p, \qquad (1.31)$$

where $0 \leqslant \theta \leqslant \pi$, $0 \leqslant \phi \leqslant 2\pi$, $0 \leqslant p < \infty$. Then intuition suggests that the measure invariant under all translations and rotations will be such that all values of p will have the same "probability" and all directions of the perpendicular. This means that the element of measure, in analogy with lines in a plane, will be given by

$$dJ = \sin\theta \, d\theta \, dp \, d\phi. \qquad (1.32)$$

Consider the representation in Cartesian coordinates which is

$$ux + vy + wz + 1 = 0, \qquad (1.33)$$

and

$$J = \int\int\int F(u,v,w)\,du\,dv\,dw.$$

The translation $x' = x + \delta t$ gives the equation

$$ux + vy + wz + 1 + u\,\delta t = 0 \qquad (1.34)$$

and on turning this into the form (1.21) the effect on the parameters is seen to be

$$u' = u - u^2\,\delta t,$$
$$v' = v - uv\,\delta t,$$
$$w' = w - uw\,\delta t. \qquad (1.35)$$

Parallel results apply for the other two translations of y and z and equations (1.19) become

$$\left(u^2\frac{\partial}{\partial u} + uv\frac{\partial}{\partial v} + uw\frac{\partial}{\partial w}\right)F = 0$$

$$\left(uv\frac{\partial}{\partial u} + v^2\frac{\partial}{\partial v} + vw\frac{\partial}{\partial w}\right)F = 0$$

$$\left(uw\frac{\partial}{\partial u} + vw\frac{\partial}{\partial v} + w^2\frac{\partial}{\partial w}\right)F = 0. \qquad (1.36)$$

In a similar manner the three infinitesimal rotations will be found to give

$$\left(w\frac{\partial}{\partial v} - v\frac{\partial}{\partial w}\right)F = 0$$

$$\left(u\frac{\partial}{\partial w} - w\frac{\partial}{\partial u}\right)F = 0$$

$$\left(v\frac{\partial}{\partial u} - u\frac{\partial}{\partial v}\right)F = 0. \qquad (1.37)$$

Using these three we get

$$u^{-1}\frac{\partial F}{\partial u} = v^{-1}\frac{\partial F}{\partial v} = w^{-1}\frac{\partial F}{\partial w} = 0 \qquad (1.38)$$

which implies, on integration, that

$$F = \phi(u^2 + v^2 + w^2).$$

The translation conditions then give

$$2\phi(u^2 + v^2 + w^2) + (u^2 + v^2 + w^2)\phi'(u^2 + v^2 + w^2) = 0 \qquad (1.39)$$

so that

$$dJ = \frac{du\,dv\,dw}{(u^2 + v^2 + w^2)^2} \qquad (1.40)$$

On transforming back to polar coordinates this becomes

$$\sin\theta \, d\theta \, dp \, d\phi$$

as conjectured. Notice the similarity of form between (1.12), (1.30) and (1.40). Pólya (1917) has shown that (1.22) is the only differential element which remains invariant under the group of all translations and rotations.

Rotations

1.19 We consider rotations around a fixed point. In two dimensions the theory is simple. A rotation is defined by an angle θ such that $0 \leqslant \theta < 2\pi$ and the sum of two rotations will be given by the sum of the corresponding θ's reduced modulo 2π. The parameter space is now bounded and it is natural to define a measure on it by a probability distribution of θ in the range $(0, 2\pi)$. The group under which the measure is to remain invariant is then naturally taken to be the rotation itself, and this forces the choice of the probability distribution which is uniform on this interval.

1.20 Rotations in three dimensions are somewhat more complicated. They may be defined either by choice of an axis of rotation and an angle through which the space or object is to be rotated, or by the choice of an orthogonal matrix representing the rotation. Here again the parameter space is bounded, and the natural group to use is the group of rotations itself. The resulting theory is described in Chapter 4.

1.21 Other classes of geometrical objects can be treated in the same way, provided we have a continuous group which is "transitive", which may be interpreted as the requirement that it is always possible to find an element of the group which will transfer any of the set of objects into any other. An example where this does not occur is given by the set of all circles in a plane when taken with the Euclidean group of all translations and rotations. It is not then possible to set up an invariant measure for this set since it is not possible to transform a circle into another circle with a different radius.

Axiomatization

1.22 Once the probability measure of a geometrical set is constituted, the solution of particular problems can proceed without the appearance of paradoxes or of difficulties touching on axiomatization. However, for the benefit of those who are more concerned with fundamentals we may note, in concluding this chapter, that A. Renyi (1955) and A. Csaszar (1955) have constructed an axiomatic theory of probability which is specially relevant to problems of geometric probability. It is based on Kolmogoroff's axiomatic foundation combined with the idea of conditional probability, which is taken as undefined.

Suppose we are given a space in which there is a σ-field $\mathscr{A}$ of sets $A, B, \ldots$ and let $\mathscr{B}$ be a sub-set of this σ-field. Then a conditional probability $P(A|B)$ is defined to be a numerical function of the two sets A and B which satisfies the following three axioms:

Axiom I. $P(A|B) \geqslant 0$, and $P(B|B) = 1$ if B belongs to $\mathscr{B}$.

Axiom II. For any fixed B, $P(A|B)$ is a measure.

Axiom III. If A and B belong to $\mathscr{A}$, and C and BC to $\mathscr{B}$, then
$$P(A|BC) P(B|C) = P(AB|C).$$

Then under wide conditions it can be shown that $P(A|B)$ can be represented in the form

$$P(A|B) = \frac{Q(AB)}{Q(B)} \tag{1.41}$$

where $Q(A)$ is a non-negative measure on the σ-field $\mathscr{A}$, and $Q(B) > 0$.

1.23 This is just the sort of thing we need in geometrical probability where we want to deal with questions such as "what is the probability that a point lies within a figure K_1 if it is known that it lies within a figure K_2" or "what is the probability that a line intersects a figure K_1 if it intersects K_2". Here the appropriate measure for random points or lines is necessarily such that it is infinite for the whole space and is therefore unsuitable for use as a probability, but the questions involve conditional distributions. Hence $M(E)$ corresponds to Renyi's measure $Q(B)$ and from it we can derive the required conditional probability distribution

$$P(E_1|E) = \frac{\displaystyle\int_{E_1 E} dM(z)}{\displaystyle\int_{E} dM(z)}$$

as in **(1.9)** A situation similar to this occurs in the application of probability to number theory.

CHAPTER 2

DISTRIBUTIONS OF POINTS IN
EUCLIDEAN SPACE

2.1   As we have shown in the last chapter, the natural measure to use for the distribution of points in a Euclidean space is Lebesgue measure, so that $M(E)$ is n-dimensional Lebesgue measure if the points are distributed in n-dimensional space.   If the number of points is to be random we suppose that the number occurring in any measurable set E is a Poisson variate with mean $\lambda M(E)$, where λ is some constant; and if the number is fixed, we suppose that the probability that it falls in a set E_1, given that it falls in $E \supset E_1$, is

$$\frac{m(EE_1)}{m(E)}.$$
(2.1)

Nearly all the problems of interest arise when $n \doteq 1$, 2, or 3, but before considering them it is convenient to prove here a general formula due to Crofton (1885) for problems involving a fixed number of points.

Crofton's theorem on fixed points

2.2   Suppose that we have N points which are independently distributed in a domain, D, in n-dimensional space.   The measure of the space (of Nn dimensions) for the joint distribution is therefore $\{m(D)\}^N$.   Suppose that we wish to calculate the probability that the figure, F, formed by the N points has a certain property which is defined in such a manner that it depends only on the relative position of the points (thus the property must be invariant under translations and rotations), and not on the domain D, or on the relative position of D and F.   For example, the property might be defined by the condition that no two of the points are more than some specified distance apart.   Then the probability that the figure F satisfies the condition is

$$P = \frac{m^*(E)}{\{m(D)\}^N},$$
(2.2)

where $m^*(E)$ is Lebesgue measure in the Nn-dimensional space, and E is the set of points in this space at which the figure F has the required property.

Write $V = m(D)$ and let D_1 be another domain containing D for which

$$m(D_1) = V + \Delta V.$$
(2.3)

Let the corresponding set in the Nn space be $E_1 \supset E$, and put

$$m^*(E) = U, \quad m^*(E_1) = U_1 = U + \Delta U.$$

Then the probability that F has the required property for random points in D_1 is

$$P_1 = P + \Delta P = \frac{U + \Delta U}{\{V + \Delta V\}^N}. \tag{2.4}$$

Consider the set E_1. This can be divided into $N+1$ sets E_{1j} ($j = 0, 1, \ldots, N$), where E_{1j} is the subset of E_1 for which j of the points lie in $D_1 - D$ and $N - j$ in D. Let P_j be the probabilities that points in E_{1j} correspond to figures in D_1 for which the required property holds. Then

$$U_1 = U + \Delta U = U + \sum_{j=1}^{N} \binom{N}{j} P_j V^{N-j} (\Delta V)^j. \tag{2.5}$$

Hence from (2.4)

$$(P + \Delta P)(V + \Delta V)^N = PV^N + \sum_{j=1}^{N} \binom{N}{j} P_j V^{N-j}(\Delta V)^j,$$

so that

$$\Delta P(V + \Delta V)^N = \sum_{j=1}^{N} \binom{N}{j} (P_j - P) V^{N-j}(\Delta V)^j. \tag{2.6}$$

We now let ΔV become small. Then to the first order, writing δP, δV for small increments, we have

$$\delta P = N(P_1 - P) V^{-1} \delta V. \tag{2.7}$$

This is *Crofton's formula*. By its use a number of awkward problems can be solved because if we can calculate P_1, which is usually much simpler, we can set up a differential equation for P in terms of some parameter which varies the measure V of the domain D.

2.3   A very simple example may be given of this method. Suppose A and B are random points on an interval of length a and we require the distribution of $x = |AB|$. Suppose the probability that $x < u$ is $F(u, a)$. Let the length of the interval have an increment δa. Then from (2.7) we have

$$\delta F(u, a) = 2(F_1(u, a) - F(u, a)) a^{-1} \delta a, \tag{2.8}$$

where $F_1(u, a)$ is the probability that $x < u$ when B is at one end of the interval. Clearly $F_1(u, a) = ua^{-1}$. Inserting this and assuming F has a differential coefficient with respect to a, we get

$$\frac{dF(u, a)}{da} + 2a^{-1} F(u, a) = 2ua^{-2},$$

so that

$$\frac{d}{da}(a^2 F(u, a)) = 2u,$$

26

and

$$a^2 F(u, a) = 2au + \text{constant.}$$

For $x = u$ we must have $F = 1$ so that the constant is $-u^2$, and

$$F(u, a) = a^{-2}\{2au - u^2\}. \tag{2.9}$$

Crofton's theorem on mean values

2.4 Further examples of this method will occur later. It may also be applied to finding the mean values of some numerical function, Y, of the F. This is a function of the N sets of coordinates in the parameter space. Let μ be the mean of Y. Then

$$\mu = WV^{-N}, \tag{2.10}$$

where $V = m(D)$, and W is the integral of Y over the Nn-dimensional product space. We now proceed as before and obtain

$$(\mu + \Delta\mu)(V + \Delta V)^N = W + W_1 + \ldots + W_N, \tag{2.11}$$

where W_k is the integral obtained by taking all cases in which there are k points in $D_1 - D$ and $N - k$ in D. We let $m(D_1 - D)$ tend to zero and we have asymptotically that

$$W_1 = N\mu_1 V^{N-1}\Delta V, \tag{2.12}$$

as $\Delta V \to 0$, whilst $W_2, \ldots, W_N$ are $o(\Delta V)$. Here μ_1 is the mean value of Y when one of the points is constrained to lie in $D_1 - D$. Hence

$$\delta\mu = N(\mu_1 - \mu) V^{-1} \delta V. \tag{2.13}$$

(2.7) can be regarded as a particular case of this which is obtained when Y is a function defined to take the values 1, 0 according as the figure F satisfies the required condition or not.

2.5 As an example consider the previous illustration where A and B are random points inside an interval of length a and we require the mean value of $x^p = |AB|^p$ $(p > 0)$. If B is at one end of the interval the mean value of x^p is

$$\mu_1 = a^{-1}\int_0^a x^p \, dx = (p+1)^{-1}a^p.$$

(2.13) then becomes

$$\delta\mu = 2\{(p+1)^{-1}a^p - \mu\}a^{-1}\delta a,$$

and integrating we obtain

$$\mu = \frac{2a^p}{(p+1)(p+2)} \tag{2.14}$$

which could have been obtained directly from the previous result.

Crofton's formulae (2.7) and (2.13) were established for random points, but the same technique could be used for more complex random elements.

Distribution of points on a line

2.6 Now consider random points on an infinite line. From the discussion above we see that this is naturally defined by ensuring that in any set of non-overlapping intervals $I_1, I_2, \dots$ the numbers of random points which occur are independent Poisson variates with means $\lambda \,|\, I_1\,|, \lambda \,|\, I_2\,|, \dots$ where λ is a constant known as the density of the distribution. Thus, given any point P, the probability that there is no random point in an interval of length a containing P, or extending from P to the right (or left), is

$$e^{-\lambda a}.$$

Hence, if P is any point, and in particular one of the random points, the probability distribution of the distance x to the nearest random point to the right (or left) is

$$dF = \lambda \, e^{-\lambda x} \, dx. \tag{2.15}$$

In the language of statistical theory we may also express this by saying that $2\lambda x$ is distributed in the χ^2 distribution with two degrees of freedom.†

2.7 We can also regard random points on a line as a realization of a "Poisson Process". Suppose that $N(a, b)$ is the number occurring in the interval (a, b) and that this has a distribution $\{P_n(a, b)\}$, $n = 0, 1, \dots$. Using the assumptions made above, we can derive differential equations for $P_n(a, b)$ by considering what may happen in an interval $(a, b+\delta)$, where δ is small. Then

$$P_n(a, b+\delta) = P_n(a, b)(1 - \lambda\delta) + P_{n-1}(a, b)\lambda\delta + o(\delta), \tag{2.16}$$

where $P_n = 0$ for $n < 0$, and we assume that the probability of a single point occurring in an interval $(b, b+\delta)$ is $\lambda\delta + o(\delta)$, independently of what happens elsewhere. Assuming that $P_n(a, b)$ is differentiable with respect to b we get

$$\frac{d}{db} P_n(a, b) = -\lambda P_n(a, b) + \lambda P_{n-1}(a, b). \tag{2.17}$$

Solving these equations for $n = 0, 1, 2, \dots$ in succession we get

$$P_n(a, b) = \{\lambda(b-a)\}^n \, e^{-\lambda(b-a)} \, (n!)^{-1}. \tag{2.18}$$

---

† We assume here and later that the reader is acquainted with the elementary distributions of statistics and with the characterization of such distributions by moments. Cf. Kendall and Stuart, vol. I, 1958.

Random division of a magnitude

2.8 A more interesting situation arises when we have a fixed number of random points in an interval whose length we may take as unity. These will divide the interval into $n+1$ random intervals which we denote in order along the line, together with their lengths, by $I_1, \ldots, I_{n+1}$. Suppose that the interval is $(0, 1)$ and that we have n random points whose coordinates $X_1, \ldots, X_n$ are independently and uniformly distributed on $(0, 1)$. Then their joint distribution can be written

$$dX_1 \ldots dX_n \, (0 \leqslant X_i \leqslant 1). \tag{2.19}$$

This can be regarded as a joint uniform distribution on an n-dimensional cube. Write $Y_1, \ldots, Y_n$ for $X_1, \ldots, X_n$ arranged in increasing order:

$$0 \leqslant Y_1 \leqslant Y_2 \leqslant \ldots \leqslant Y_n \leqslant 1.$$

Then the cube is divided into $n!$ equal regions in which the density is uniform, and the joint distribution of the Y_i is given by

$$n! \, dY_1 \ldots dY_n \, (0 \leqslant Y_1 \leqslant \ldots \leqslant Y_n \leqslant 1). \tag{2.20}$$

We then have

$$I_1 = Y_1,$$
$$I_2 = Y_2 - Y_1,$$

$$\cdot \quad \cdot \quad \cdot \quad \cdot \quad \cdot$$

$$I_n = Y_n - Y_{n-1},$$
$$I_{n+1} = 1 - Y_n.$$

The joint distribution of $I_1, \ldots, I_{n+1}$ is singular since $\Sigma I_i = 1$, but we can determine the joint distribution of $I_1, \ldots, I_n$ which, by calculating the Jacobian, is seen to be

$$n! \, dI_1 \ldots dI_n \quad (\sum_i^n I_i \leqslant 1) \tag{2.21}$$

Each interval considered by itself therefore has the same distribution. This could also have been seen by observing that the $n+1$ intervals are jointly distributed in the same way as the $n+1$ intervals obtained by placing $n+1$ points at random on a circle of unit circumference.

2.9 To determine the distribution of a single interval consider $I_{k+1} = Y_{k+1} - Y_k$. Integrating (2.21) over the possible values of $Y_1, \ldots, Y_{k-1}$ and $Y_{k+2}, \ldots Y_n$ we get

$$dF = \frac{n! X_k^{k-1} (1 - X_{k+1})^{n-k-1}}{k-1! \, n-k-1!} \, dY_k \, dY_{k+1}, \, (0 \leqslant Y_k \leqslant Y_{k+1} \leqslant 1), \tag{2.22}$$

for the joint distribution of Y_k and Y_{k+1}, and hence the distribution of I_{k+1} is

$$dI_{k+1}\, \frac{n!}{k-1!\,n-k-1!} \int_0^{1-I_{k+1}} x^{k-1}\,(1-I_{k+1}-x)^{n-k-1}\,dx$$

$$= dI_{k+1}\, \frac{n!\,(1-I_{k+1})^{n-1}}{k-1!\,n-k-1!} \int_0^1 w^{k-1}\,(1-w)^{n-k-1}\,dw,$$

$$= n\,(1-I_{k+1})^{n-1}\,dI_{k+1}. \tag{2.23}$$

This is independent of k and could have been obtained directly by observing that all the I's have the same distribution, and (2.23) is obviously the distribution of I_1.

2.10 We can relate the distribution of n points in an interval to a Poisson process in two ways. Suppose first that we have a Poisson process starting from zero and such that events happen at times $Y_1, Y_2, \ldots,$ $(0 \leqslant Y_i < \infty)$. We consider the conditional distribution of $Y_1, \ldots, Y_n$ conditional on $Y_n < 1$, $Y_{n+1} > 1$ and show that in these circumstances the n points $Y_1, \ldots, Y_n$ are n points distributed at random in $(0, 1)$ and rearranged in order. The probability that $Y_1, \ldots, Y_n$ are such that $Y_n < 1$, $Y_{n+1} > 1$ and have specified values is given by

$$\prod_1^n \lambda e^{-\lambda I_i}\,dI_i \exp -\lambda\left(1 - \sum_1^n I_i\right) = \prod_1^n \lambda^n e^{-\lambda}\,dI_i, \tag{2.24}$$

where the I_i are defined as before. The conditional probability will be obtained by dividing this expression by its integral over the region $\sum_1^n I_i \leqslant 1$ which is clearly

$$(n!)^{-1}\,\lambda^n\,e^{-\lambda}, \tag{2.25}$$

and the joint distribution of the I_i is therefore

$$n!\,dI_1 \ldots dI_n \qquad (\Sigma I_i \leqslant 1), \tag{2.26}$$

so that the joint distribution of the Y_i is

$$n!\,dY_1 \ldots dY_n, \tag{2.27}$$

which shows that the points $Y_1, \ldots, Y_n$ may be regarded as n random points in the interval $(0, 1)$.

2.11 We can also obtain a different representation which is more useful in some problems. Consider again a Poisson process with events occurring at times $Y_1, \ldots, Y_n, Y_{n+1}, \ldots,$ and write

$$Z_1 = Y_1\,Y_{n+1}^{-1},$$
$$Z_2 = Y_2\,Y_{n+1}^{-1}$$
$$\cdot \quad \cdot \quad \cdot \quad \cdot \quad \cdot$$
$$Z_n = Y_n\,Y_{n+1}^{-1}. \tag{2.28}$$

Then $0 \leqslant Z_i \leqslant 1$ and $Z_1, \ldots, Z_n$ are distributed in the interval $(0, 1)$ as an ordered set of n random points. To see this we observe that the joint distribution of $Y_1, \ldots, Y_{n+1}$ is $(Y_1 \leqslant \ldots \leqslant Y_{n+1})$

$$\lambda^{n+1} \exp - \lambda \, Y_{n+1} \, dY_1 \ldots dY_{n+1}, \tag{2.29}$$

whilst the distribution of Y_{n+1} by itself is

$$(n!)^{-1} \, Y_{n+1}^n \, \lambda^{n+1} \exp - \lambda Y_{n+1} \, dY_{n+1}. \tag{2.30}$$

Thus the conditional distribution of $Y_1, \ldots, Y_n$ given Y_{n+1} is

$$(n!)^{-1} \, Y_{n+1}^{-n} \, dX_1 \ldots dX_n, \tag{2.31}$$

and changing to Z's this becomes

$$(n!)^{-1} dZ_1 \ldots dZ_n. \tag{2.32}$$

Another representation is useful. Since $Y_i - Y_{i-1}$ is distributed as $(2\lambda)^{-1} \chi^2$ with two degrees of freedom the joint distribution of $I_1, \ldots, I_{n+1}$ is that of the quantities

$$(x_{2i-1}^2 + x_{2i}^2) \left(\sum_{s=1}^{2n+2} x_s^2 \right)^{-1}, \quad i = 1, \ldots, n+1, \tag{2.33}$$

where the x_i are independent random variables which are distributed normally with zero means and the same standard deviation.

2.12 Since the joint distribution of the intervals $I_1, \ldots I_{n+1}$ is the same as that of the $n+1$ quantities

$$W_1(W_1 + \ldots + W_{n+1})^{-1}, \ldots, W_{n+1}(W_1 + \ldots + W_{n+1})^{-1}, \quad \text{say,}$$

where the W_i are independently distributed in the same negative exponential distribution, we can give the joint distribution of the I_i another geometrical interpretation. Regard $(W_1, \ldots, W_{n+1})$ as a point in $(n+1)$-dimensional space. The I_i depend only on the ratios of the W_i, and the probability density of the joint distribution of the W_i depends only on ΣW_i. It is therefore constant on the plane $\Sigma W_i = 1$. This plane cuts the positive part of the space in a regular simplex. This is the n-dimensional generalization of the equilateral triangle, regular tetrahedron, etc. If we now transfer our attention to this n-dimensional space for some fixed value of ΣW_i and choose a scale such that the distance of each vertex from the opposite side is unity, the joint distribution of $I_1, \ldots, I_{n+1}$ is that of the lengths of the $n+1$ perpendiculars from a random point inside the simplex on the $n+1$ sides.

The advantage of this representation is that one can sometimes obtain explicit formulae for probabilities by using the geometry of a simplex. On the other hand, the advantage of (2.33) is that it simplifies the calculation of moments. To illustrate this consider the expression ((2.33)):

$$\frac{x_1^2 + x_2^2}{x_1^2 + \ldots + x_{2n}^2} = \frac{A}{B}. \tag{2.34}$$

The distribution of A/B depends only on the ratios of the x_i. Since the joint distribution of $x_1, \ldots x_{2n}$ is spherically symmetric, the distributions of A/B and B are independent and hence

$$E\left\{\left(\frac{A}{B}\right)^n B^n\right\} = E(A^n),$$

and thus

$$E\left(\frac{A}{B}\right)^n = \frac{E(A^n)}{E(B^n)}, \quad (n > 0). \tag{2.35}$$

This greatly simplifies the finding of moments.

Some special problems

2.13   We can now consider a series of particular problems of which a large number, mostly very special, have been constructed. Thus, suppose a unit interval is divided into three parts by two points at random and we ask for the probability that it is possible to construct a triangle having these subintervals as sides. The required probability is the probability that no one of the intervals is greater than the sum of the other two. Using the simplicial representation, which is here a triangle, the region in which the representative point must lie for a triangle to be possible is the region inside the triangle formed by joining the midpoints of the sides as illustrated in Fig. (2.1).

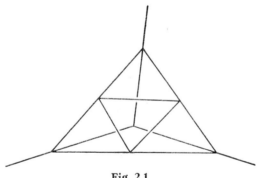

Fig. 2.1

This has an area equal to one quarter of the larger triangle so that the probability is $\frac{1}{4}$.

The largest interval on a line

2.14   A more interesting problem is to determine the distribution of the largest of the n intervals found by $n-1$ random points in a unit interval. The probability that the largest interval is greater than x, say, is the complement of the probability that no interval is greater than x. Let us find more generally the probability that exactly k intervals are greater than x, where $k = 0, 1, \ldots$, and $kx \leqslant 1$. In a simplified form this problem was originally given by Whitworth (1901, Problem 667, p. 361) but is possibly earlier in origin. We shall prove that the probability is

$$P_{[k]} = \binom{n}{k}\left\{(1-kx)^{n-1} - \binom{n-1}{1}(1-(k+1)x)^{n-1} + \ldots \right.$$
$$\left. + (-)^s\binom{n-k}{s}(1-(k+s)x)^{n-1}\right\}, \quad (2.36)$$

where the series stops at the last term for which $1-(k+s)x$ is positive.

Let the intervals be numbered $I_1, \ldots, I_n$ and write $P_{ij\ldots k}$ for the probability that $I_i > x$, $I_j > x$, $\ldots I_k > x$, whatever the size of the other intervals. Let S_m be the sum of $P_{ij\ldots k}$ for all selections of m out of the n intervals. Then if the events $E_1, \ldots, E_n$ are defined to be the events that $I_1 > x, \ldots, I_n > x$, a well-known combinatorial theorem states that the probability that exactly k of these events occur is

$$P_{[k]} = S_k - \binom{k+1}{k}S_{k+1} + \binom{k+2}{k}S_{k+2} - \ldots.$$

This may be easily established by using indicator variates (equal to $1, 0$ according as an event does or does not occur) or by induction (Feller, 1950).

S_m is clearly $\binom{n}{m}$ times the probability that $I_1 > x, \ldots, I_m > x$, and using the geometrical representation of the I_i as perpendiculars on the faces of an $(n-1)$-dimensional simplex we see that this is obtained by finding the volume of a regular simplex all of whose sides are reduced in ratio $(1-mx)$. Hence S_m is equal to

$$\binom{n}{m}(1-mx)^{n-1},$$

if $0 < mx < 1$ and is zero otherwise. Then $P_{[k]}$ is given by

$$\sum_{s=0}\binom{k+s}{s}(-)^s\binom{n}{s}(1-sx)^{n-1},$$

which is equal to (2.36).

This gives the distribution of the largest interval on putting $k = 0$ since $P_{[0]}$ is the probability that the largest is less than x. This is

$$P_{[0]} = 1 - \binom{n}{1}(1-x)^{n-1} + \binom{n}{2}(1-2x)^{n-1} - \ldots \quad (2.37)$$

The probability that the largest exceeds x is then

$$1 - P_{[0]} = \binom{n}{1}(1-x)^{n-1} - \binom{n}{2}(1-2x)^{n-1} + \ldots \quad (2.38)$$

2.15 These results were also obtained by Fisher (1929, 1940) for use as a test of significance in harmonic analysis. Both of these papers were reproduced in his collected papers with additions, and in the first of these he gives a table of the 5% and 1% points of (2.38) for $n = 5 (1) 50$. In the second paper he also gives the 5% points of the second largest interval for $n = 3 (1) 10 (5) 50$. In Davis (1941) there is a table for $nx = 0\cdot1 (0\cdot1) 10\cdot0$, $n = 10 (10) 70$ and for $nx = 5\cdot1 (0\cdot1) 10\cdot0$, $n = 80 (10) 300$. These formulae have been applied by F. Garwood (1940) to the theory of the operation of vehicular controlled traffic lights, and he also gives another proof. The problem has also been discussed by Baticle (1933a, 1933b, 1935) and Lévy (1939).

2.16 A geometrical problem of an apparently different kind has been considered by Stevens (1939) but, as Fisher (1940) points out, it is exactly equivalent. On the circumference of a circle of length unity n arcs of length x are placed at random and we ask for the probability that the circumference is completely covered. Consider the arcs as being determined by their most clockwise points. These determine n intervals whose joint distribution is that of the n intervals formed by $n-1$ random points in an interval of unit length. If, and only if, none of these lengths is greater than x, all the points of the circumference are covered. A proof of the result in this form was given by Stevens. Mauldon (1951) has given the exact distribution of the sum of the m largest intervals for $m = 2, 3, \ldots$

2.17 Stevens' problem is about a set of random intervals on a circle. The analogous problem in three dimensions is that of finding the probability that the surface of a sphere is completely covered by a set of randomly placed circles. No exact solution is known, but the problem and its biological origin will be discussed in Chapter 5.

2.18 Another problem of some interest is the distribution of ΣI_n^2. This was originally proposed as a test of significance for the statistical study of infectious diseases by M. Greenwood (1946). The exact distribution, like the one in **2.14**, is analytic only in strips and is known exactly for $n = 2, 3, 4$ only. The moments and the asymptotic form are given by Moran (1947) and the solution for $n = 4$ by Gardner (1952) (see also Moran (1951, 1953)). The moments are not difficult to find, either by using the representation (2.35) or by using a theorem of Dirichlet (Whittaker and Watson (1935), p. 258).

If $f(x)$ is integrable on the range $(0, 1)$ and $\alpha_r > 0\,(r = 1, \ldots, n)$ then

$$\int \ldots \int f(x_1 + \ldots + x_n)\, x_1^{\alpha_1 - 1} \ldots x_n^{\alpha_n - 1}\, dx_1 \ldots dx_n \qquad (2.39)$$

taken over the region $x_i \geqslant 0$, $\Sigma x_i \leqslant 1$, is equal to

$$\frac{\Gamma(\alpha_1)\dots\Gamma(\alpha_n)}{\Gamma(\alpha_1+\dots+\alpha_n)}\int_0^1 f(t)\, t^{\Sigma\alpha_i-1}\, dt. \tag{2.40}$$

This is easily proved by successive reduction. In particular, if $f(t)$ is equal to unity, (2.39) is equal to

$$\frac{\Gamma(\alpha_1)\dots\Gamma(\alpha_n)}{\Gamma(\alpha_1+\dots+\alpha_n+1)}. \tag{2.41}$$

If the integral was taken over the range $0 \leqslant \Sigma x_i \leqslant C$ it would be multiplied by $C^{\Sigma\alpha_i}$, and differentiating with respect to C we see that the integral of

$$x_1^{\alpha_1-1}\dots x_n^{\alpha_n-1}$$

over the $(n-1)$-dimensional region defined by $x_i \geqslant 0, \Sigma x_i = 1$, is equal to

$$\frac{\Gamma(\alpha_1)\dots\Gamma(\alpha_n)}{\Gamma(\alpha_1+\dots+\alpha_n)}. \tag{2.42}$$

Putting $\alpha_1 = \dots = \alpha_n = 1$ we obtain the volume of this region to be equal to $\Gamma(n)^{-1}$, and then, using the representation of the n intervals formed by $n-1$ random points as the homogeneous coordinates of points inside the simplex, as explained before, we find that

$$E(I_1^{\alpha_1-1}\dots I_n^{\alpha_n-1}) = \frac{\Gamma(n)\,\Gamma(\alpha_1)\dots\Gamma(\alpha_n)}{\Gamma(\alpha_1+\dots+\alpha_n)}. \tag{2.43}$$

This was originally obtained in a very slightly different form by Whitworth (1901) (Proposition LVII). Applying this to the sum $T = \sum_1^n I_i^2$ we get

$$E(T) = nE(I_1^2) = 2(n+1)^{-1}, \tag{2.44}$$

$$E(T^2) = nE(I_1^4) + n(n-1)E(I_1^2 I_2^2)$$
$$= 4(n+5)\{(n+1)(n+2)(n+3)\}^{-1}, \tag{2.45}$$

and so on.

2.19   The distributions considered above can both be used as a test for the hypothesis that the $n-1$ points are in fact distributed at random. Another such test was suggested by Bartlett in the discussion on Greenwood's paper (1946, p. 108). Since we have shown above that $I_1, \dots, I_n$ are distributed as $W_i(W_1+\dots+W_n)^{-1}$ $(i = 1, \dots, n)$ where the W_i are independent random variables distributed as χ^2 with two degrees of freedom, we could use any standard test for the homogeneity of variances. In particular a likelihood ratio test must be based on some function of

$$\frac{\prod\limits_{i=1}^{n} I_i^{1/n}}{\sum\limits_{i=1}^{n} I_i}.$$

(2.46)

The distribution of this quantity has been extensively studied (for references see, for example, Kendall and Stuart (1958)).

Kolmogoroff's test

2.20 The theory of the distribution of random points in an interval is also related to another classical problem in mathematical statistics, that of the goodness-of-fit of a sample to a postulated theoretical probability distribution. Suppose that $F(x)$ is a probability distribution which is continuous, i.e. has no discrete component. If $x_1, ..., x_n$ is a sample in order of magnitude, from this distribution, define the sample distribution function, $F_n(x)$, by

$$\begin{aligned} F_n(x) &= 0, \quad x \leqslant x_1, \\ &= kn^{-1}, \quad x_k < x \leqslant x_{k+1}, \\ &= 1, \quad x_n < x, \end{aligned}$$

(2.47)

and the divergence from the theoretical distribution by

$$D_n = \text{least upper bound } |F_n(x) - F(x)|.$$

(2.48)

The advantage of this criterion of divergence between $F(x)$ and $F_n(x)$ is that it remains invariant when x is made to undergo any continuous monotonic transformation. We can therefore suppose that

$$\begin{aligned} F(x) &= 0, \quad x < 0, \\ &= x, \quad 0 \leqslant x \leqslant 1, \\ &= 1, \quad x > 1. \end{aligned}$$

(2.49)

The sample is then that of n random points in an interval and in the notation used before,

$$D_n = \max_{1 < i < n} \max \{|Y_i - in^{-1}|, |Y_i - (i-1)n^{-1}|\}.$$

(2.50)

Kolmogoroff (1933) proves that for $x > 0$,

$$\lim_{n \to \infty} \Pr \{n^{\frac{1}{2}} D_n \leqslant x\} = 1 - 2 \sum_{v=1}^{\infty} (-1)^{v-1} e^{-2v^2 x^2},$$

(2.51)

the right-hand side being a Jacobian theta function. This distribution has an extensive literature, since D_n has a wide application as a test of goodness of fit (it should, however, be noticed that the above result does not hold for distributions fitted to the sample by estimating parameters).† The other distributions discussed above could also be used

† See Kendall and Stuart, vol. II, 1961.

in this manner as tests of goodness of fit but, unlike Kolmogoroff's test, require the transformation to a rectangular distribution to be carried out before the test is applied.

2.21 Considered as tests of significance, the relative values of all such distributions must depend on the alternative hypotheses envisaged. Thus in the epidemiological problem considered by Greenwood, Moran has shown (1951) that for a very plausible alternative Bartlett's method using a homogeneity of variance test is better than the use of $\Sigma \mid I_i \mid^2$. A particularly valuable and interesting survey of these and other tests, and of their powers, is given by Cox (1955).

Non-overlapping intervals on a line

2.22 Next suppose that, instead of considering random points on a line, we try to define random non-overlapping intervals. Consider first an infinite range. The occurrence of non-overlapping intervals could be regarded as the realisation of a random process in which t is the time coordinate on the range $(-\infty, \infty)$. If there is no interval covering a point t we may suppose that the distribution of the length, T_1 say, to the nearest interval on the right is distributed in a negative exponential distribution,

$$\lambda e^{-\lambda T_1} dT_1 \tag{2.52}$$

with mean λ^{-1}, independently of what happens to the left of t_1. If the interval then beginning has the constant length δ, the line will again be uncovered at $t + T_1 + \delta$, and the distance to the next interval is again a negative exponential variate T_2 with mean λ^{-1}. Carrying on in the same way we thus define a random process. This type of model occurs in a number of practical situations. Thus it may be applied to represent the distribution of traffic along a road, or passing a given point during a period of time. However, in this case, if δ is taken as the length of a car, the model appears to be satisfactory only when the traffic density is quite low. Better results may be had if δ is taken as larger than the car length.

The model can also represent the intervals during which telephone conversations are held on a line from a single subscriber, provided there is never any blockage and the holding time of each conversation is a constant equal to δ.

Finally the model can also represent the sequence of intervals during which a counter is occupied when it is actuated by a random sequence of events, such as the passage of cosmic ray particles, and is such that after registering each event the counter is insensitive for a period δ.

All three of these subjects have extensive literatures which are not really relevant to the subject of geometrical probability, and we consider here only one problem which arises in this model.

2.23 Supposing that at time $t = 0$ there is no interval occurring, and we wish to know the distribution of the total number of intervals which lie within the interval $(0, T)$. This is most easily done by finding the probability that n or more intervals are contained in $(0, T)$. The end of the nth interval will occur at $n\delta + T_1 + \ldots + T_n$ where the T_i are independently distributed as $(2\lambda)^{-1}\chi^2$ with two degrees of freedom, and n or more intervals will occur in $(0, T)$ if $T_1 + \ldots + T_n \leqslant T - n\delta$. The probability of this happening is therefore

$$\Pr\{\chi^2_{(2n)} \leqslant 2\lambda(T - n\delta)\}$$

$$= 2^{-n}\,\Gamma(n)^{-1} \int_0^{2\lambda(T - n\delta)} e^{-\frac{1}{2}x}\, x^{n-1}\, dx. \tag{2.53}$$

Clearly more than $[T(n\delta)^{-1}]$ intervals cannot occur, where $[x]$ is the integral part of x (compare Frenkel, 1946, p. 128).

2.24 If we are to have exactly n intervals in $(0, T)$ the joint distribution of their positions may be defined in various ways. Suppose that the intervals are of length δ and that there are n of them. These will leave $n+1$ random intervals $I_1, \ldots, I_{n+1}$ uncovered, and we may suppose that these are jointly distributed as the $n+1$ intervals formed in an interval of length $T - n\delta$ by n points placed at random. From (2.21) this joint distribution is

$$(T - n\delta)^{-n}(n+1)!\, dI_1 \ldots dI_n \quad \left(\sum_1^n I_i \leqslant 1\right). \tag{2.54}$$

Another definition which is not equivalent to this is to suppose that the intervals of length δ are placed in the interval $(0, T)$ successively, at each stage all possible positions being taken as equally probable. In this case it is always possible to put a number n in the interval $(0, T)$ where n is defined to be equal to $[T(2\delta)^{-1}]$ if $[T\delta^{-1}]$ is even, and $[T(2\delta)^{-1}]+1$ if $[T\delta^{-1}]$ is odd. However, if the positions are properly chosen we may be able to put in up to $[T\delta^{-1}]$ intervals. Thus if we continue to insert intervals until no more can be inserted the total number will be a random variable whose distribution depends on T. The determination of this problem is a matter of some difficulty for which see Renyi (1958). A discrete analogue of this problem has been studied by E. S. Page (1959) (see also Downton, 1961) and this has some interesting physical applications when generalized to two dimensions.

Density of points in a plane

2.25 Now consider random numbers of points in a plane so that the number occurring in any region of area A is a Poisson variate with mean λA. λ may then be called the "density" of the points. Let P be any point and $r_1, r_2, \ldots$ be the distances to the nearest, second nearest, and so on. The distribution of r_1 is then clearly

$$2\lambda\pi r_1 \exp - \lambda\pi r_1^2 . dr_1, \tag{2.55}$$

so that $2\lambda\pi r_1^2$ is distributed as χ^2 with two degrees of freedom. Similarly r_s will have the distribution

$$2(\lambda\pi)^s (s-1!)^{-1} \exp - \lambda\pi r_s^2 . r_s^{2s-1} dr_s, \tag{2.56}$$

so that $2\lambda\pi r_s^2$ is distributed as χ^2 with $2s$ degrees of freedom. In fact the joint distribution of the quantities $r_1^2, r_2^2, r_3^2, \ldots$ is that of the distances of the nearest, second nearest, and so on points, on the right-hand side of a given point on a line on which random points are occurring with density $\lambda\pi$. This equivalence can be seen directly.

2.26 These results may be used to provide a means of estimating the density of points in a plane by choosing random points and measuring distances to the sth nearest neighbour. The mean value of r_s^2 is therefore $s(\lambda\pi)^{-1}$ and, if we are going to use a number of such estimates, it is better to add them together and take the mean as an estimate of λ^{-1} rather than add a number of biassed estimators of λ. Suppose that $y_1, \ldots, y_n$ are n values of r_1^2 and $Y = n^{-1}(y_1 + \ldots + y_n)$. Then the expectation of Y is $(\lambda\pi)^{-1}$ so that πY is an unbiassed estimator of λ^{-1} and its variance is easily seen to be $(n\lambda^2)^{-1}$. As an estimate of λ we may therefore take $\lambda_1 = (\pi Y)^{-1}$ and for n large this will have a variance $\lambda^2 n^{-1}$. Furthermore $2\lambda n\pi Y$ will be distributed as χ^2 with $2n$ degrees of freedom, so confidence limits for λ are easily found.

In practice $2r_1$ is often used to estimate $\lambda^{-\frac{1}{2}}$ instead of πr_1^2 to estimate λ^{-1}. From (2.55) we easily see that the mean of $2r_1$ is $\lambda^{-\frac{1}{2}}$ and its variance is $\pi^{-1}(4-\pi)\lambda^{-1}$. When a sum of $2r_1$'s is used to provide an estimate of λ the efficiency of the procedure, relative to using r_1^2, is therefore $\pi\{4(4-\pi)\}^{-1} = 0.9149$.

2.27 Applications of this result and various modifications of it have been used in estimating the densities of plants and trees, and the reader interested in the practical aspects should consult Greig-Smith (1957), Moore (1954), Cottam (1947), Cottam and Curtis (1949, 1955, 1956), Cottam, Curtis and Hale (1953), Morisita (1954), Clark and Evans (1954, 1955), and Shanks (1954).

2.28 Some of these references do not show a very clear idea of the background theory, and a wide variety of modifications of such methods has been proposed without much theoretical analysis. In addition to the above method, which is known as the closest individual method, four other methods will now be considered briefly as illustrating how the theory of geometrical probability may be applied.

(1) Instead of choosing a point P other than one of the given set of random points (say, trees), we choose at random one of that set, and measure the distance to its nearest neighbour. The distribution is then the same as before.

(2) As in the first method, a point P is chosen at random independently of the given points. Let Q_1 be its nearest neighbour, and Q_2 the nearest neighbour to Q_1. The distance Q_1Q_2 is used to provide an estimate of λ. It has several times been stated that this has the same distribution as in the previous case, but this is quite incorrect, and we calculate its distribution as an illustration of the methods which can be applied in such problems. Let r be the distance PQ_1, and R the radius of a circle about Q_1 (Fig. 2.2). Then r has the distribution

$$2\lambda\pi r\,e^{-\lambda\pi r^2}\,dr, \tag{2.57}$$

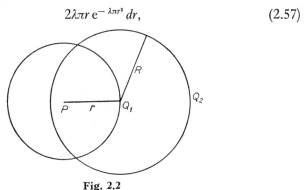

Fig. 2.2

and, conditional on the value of r, the probability that there is no random point inside a circle of radius R about the point Q_1 is

$$e^{-\lambda A(r,\,R)}, \tag{2.58}$$

where $A(r, R)$ is the area of the region inside the circle of centre Q_1 but outside the circle of centre P. Then the distribution of x, the distance of Q_1 to its nearest neighbour, is

$$2\lambda\pi\,dx \int_0^\infty r\,\frac{d}{dx}\,e^{-\lambda\pi r^2 - \lambda A(r,\,R)}\,dr. \tag{2.59}$$

This is awkward to evaluate explicitly, but the mean of Q_1Q_2 is not difficult to find. This is

$$2\lambda\pi \int_0^\infty \int_0^\infty rx\,\frac{d}{dx}\,e^{-\lambda\pi r^2 - \lambda A(r,\,R)}\,dr\,dx. \tag{2.60}$$

A is equal to

$$\pi R^2 - r^2\{\theta - \sin\theta\cos\theta\} - R^2\{\phi - \sin\phi\cos\phi\},$$

where

$$\theta = \cos^{-1}(1 - R^2(2r^2)^{-1}),$$
$$\phi = \cos^{-1}R(2r)^{-1}.$$

By partial integration (2.60) becomes

$$\lambda^{-\frac{1}{2}} \int_0^\infty \frac{dy}{\{1 + \pi^{-1}A(1, y)\}^{\frac{3}{2}}}, \tag{2.61}$$

which can be shown by numerical integration to equal $1 \cdot 191\lambda^{-\frac{1}{2}}$. Thus $0 \cdot 8396r$ is an unbiassed estimate of $\lambda^{-\frac{1}{2}}$ and its variance could be calculated in a similar manner.

(3) A random sampling point P is chosen and the nearest, Q_1, of the random points is found. The distance, r, of Q_1 from the nearest point Q_2 to Q_1 on the other side of a line through P perpendicular to PQ_1 Fig. 2.3) is measured.

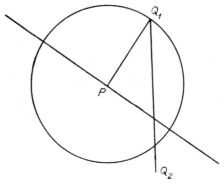

Fig. 2.3

The mean of the distribution of Q_1Q_2 could then be found by a similar kind of argument to that used above, but the calculations would be somewhat more complicated.

(4) A random point P is chosen together with two perpendicular directions fixed in advance. The distances, y_1, y_2, y_3, y_4, say, of P from the nearest random point in each of the four quadrants are measured. From what has gone before we see that $\frac{1}{2}\lambda\pi y_i^2 (i = 1, ..., 4)$ are distributed independently as χ^2 with two degrees of freedom. Hence

$$\tfrac{1}{16}\pi(y_1^2 + y_2^2 + y_3^2 + y_4^2)$$

is an unbiassed estimator of λ^{-1}, with variance $\frac{1}{4}\lambda^{-2}$, and confidence limits can be established as before. In ecological literature it is usual to use the mean of the distances and not their squares, but, as shown before, this is inefficient.

2.29 The reasons why such a variety of methods should have been suggested and used is not clear. Methods (2) and (3) are involved mathematically, their standard errors have not been calculated, and they must entail more labour. The best procedure appears to be to take random sampling points and measure the distance to the nearest, or sth nearest neighbours. If the points are not distributed at random all these methods will give biassed results, but the theory of such non-random distributions lies outside the scope of this book.

Distribution of the distance of two points in a circle

2.30 As an example of problems involving a fixed number of points consider first the distribution of the distance between two points taken inside a circle. This has been obtained by a number of different writers and the easiest method appears to be the use of Crofton's theorem.

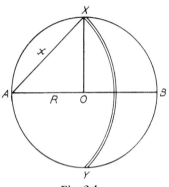

Fig. 2.4

We first obtain the mean of the distance between two points P, Q, each distributed uniformly over a circle of radius R (Fig. 2.4).

Let A be a point on the circumference and AOB the diameter. The points distant x from A in the elemental arc XY occupy an element of area equal to $\left(2x\cos^{-1}\dfrac{x}{2R}\right)dx$ and hence the mean distance from A is given by

$$\frac{1}{\pi R^2}\int_0^{2R} 2x^2\cos^{-1}\frac{x}{2R}\,dx = \frac{16R}{\pi}\int_0^{\frac{\pi}{2}}\theta\cos^2\theta\sin\theta\,d\theta = \frac{32R}{9\pi}. \tag{2.62}$$

Let $M(R)$ be the mean distance. Then using (2.13) we have

$$\frac{dM(R)}{dR} = 2\left\{\frac{32R}{9\pi} - M(R)\right\}\frac{2}{R}. \tag{2.63}$$

Multiplying by R^4 and integrating, we obtain

$$M(R)R^4 = \frac{128R^5}{45} + \text{constant.}$$

Since $M(R)$ must equal zero when $R = 0$, we have

$$M(R) = \frac{128}{45}R. \tag{2.64}$$

Now let $p(x, R)\,dx$ be the probability that PQ lies in the interval $(x, x+dx)$. Then $p_1(x, R)$, the same probability when P lies on the circumference, is

$$2\theta x\,(\pi R^2)^{-1},$$

where $\theta = \cos^{-1} x\,(2R)^{-1}$. For fixed x we have

$$\tan\theta\,d\theta = R^{-1}\,dR,$$

so that (2.7) becomes

$$\frac{dp}{d\theta} + 4p\tan\theta = \frac{32\theta}{\pi x}\sin\theta\cos\theta, \qquad (2.65)$$

and the general integral of this equation is

$$p = \frac{16}{\pi x}\{\theta\sin^2\theta\cos^2\theta - \sin\theta\cos^3\theta + \theta\cos^4\theta\} + \lambda\cos^4\theta, \qquad (2.66)$$

where λ is a constant. Since $p = 0$ when $\theta = 0$ we have

$$p = \frac{16}{\pi x}\{\theta\sin^2\theta\cos^2\theta - \sin\theta\cos^3\theta + \theta\cos^4\theta\}$$

$$= \frac{8}{\pi R}\{\theta\sin^2\theta\cos\theta - \sin\theta\cos^2\theta + \theta\cos^3\theta\},$$

and integrating this we get

$$p(x, R) = \frac{1}{\pi R^2}\{\pi x^2 + (R^2 - x^2)(\pi - 2\alpha) - \tfrac{1}{2}(2R^2 + x^2)\sin 2\alpha\} \qquad (2.67)$$

where $x = 2R\cos\alpha$.

The same result could have been obtained by a direct calculation. This is done by Borel (1925) who considers the analogous problems when P and Q are random points inside triangles, squares, and polygons in general. Clearly the distribution of PQ and its moments can be regarded as still another of the many numbers which can be used to characterize convex domains in two dimensions (or analogously, convex domains in a higher number of dimensions).

Sylvester's problem

2.31 A more difficult problem is that known as Sylvester's. This is the problem of finding the probability that four points A, B, C, D, taken at random inside a convex domain, form a convex quadrilateral, i.e. none of the points is inside the triangle formed by the other three. Consider the complementary probability that the quadrilateral is not convex. This can occur in four different ways, according to which of the four points occurs inside the triangle formed by the other three. If the domain has area S and the mean area of the triangle is T, the probability of a convex quadrilateral is

$$1 - 4TS^{-1}. \qquad (2.68)$$

Since P is unaffected by the scale of the domain in which the four points lie, and since this domain is convex, we can imagine it included in a larger domain of the same shape and orientation. Hence using (2.13) it follows that $dP = 0$ and hence that $P = P_1$, where P_1 is the probability of the quadrilateral being convex when one of its points is constrained to lie at random in the added infinitesimal part of the domain. Arguing as before, we then have

$$P_1 = 1 - 3T_1 S^{-1}, \qquad (2.69)$$

where T_1 is the mean area of a triangle one of whose points lies on the boundary, this mean value being averaged over all possible positions of the boundary point weighted by the amount by which the domain is increased there. We now get a factor 3 instead of 4 because only three free vertices may be chosen at random.

The following argument could be carried out directly for any convex figure, but for the sake of simplicity we stick to the traditional exposition in terms of a convex polygon, one of whose vertices is the point, A say, which is the fixed vertex of the polygon. Let there be n vertices in all and join A to the other $n-1$ vertices, thus forming $n-1$ triangles whose areas are $S_1, ..., S_{n-1}$ (Fig. 2.5).

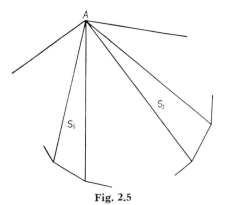

Fig. 2.5

Let T_{ij} be the mean area of a triangle of whose vertices one is A and the other two are points taken at random in the triangles i and j (where $i = j$ or $i \neq j$). Then

$$\left(\sum_{i=1}^{n-1} S_i\right)^2 T_1 = \sum_{i=1}^{n-1} S_i^2 T_{ii} + \sum_{\substack{i,j=1 \\ i \neq j}}^{n-1} S_i S_j T_{ij}. \qquad (2.70)$$

Suppose first that $i \neq j$, and B is a random point in S_i, C a random point in S_j. If B is kept fixed, the mean area of the triangle ABC is clearly ABG_j, where G_j is the centre of gravity of the triangle j. Then varying B the mean value of ABC is AG_iG_j.

If $i = j$ we first notice that T_{ii} must be of the form λS_i, where λ is independent of the shape and size of S_i. This follows because we can transform any triangle into any other triangle by projecting from one plane perpendicularly on to another and then changing the scale. In doing this the areas of S_i and ABC are multiplied by the same factor, and the probabilities of points lying in corresponding regions remain equal. If AXY is any triangle, W the middle point of XY, G_1, G_2 the centres of gravity of AXW, AWY, and S the area of AXY, we get

$$S^2 \lambda S = 2(\tfrac{1}{2}S)^2 \lambda \tfrac{1}{2}S + \tfrac{1}{2}S^2(AG_1G_2). \tag{2.71}$$

Moreover AG_1G_2 is easily seen to be $\tfrac{2}{9}S$. Hence, solving for λ we get

$$\lambda = \frac{4}{27}$$

so that
$$T_{ii} = \frac{4}{27}S_i. \tag{2.72}$$

2.32 By proceeding to the limit, (2.70) can be turned into an integral for any convex region (Fig. 2.6). Suppose that A is a point on the

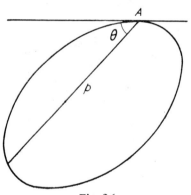

Fig. 2.6

boundary of the region and the region is defined by the function $p(\theta)\,(0 \leqslant \theta \leqslant \pi)$, where $p(\theta)$ is the distance of the boundary from A along a line making an angle θ with a tangent at A. Then (2.70) becomes

$$S^2 T_1 = \tfrac{1}{18} \int_0^\pi \int_0^\pi p(\theta)^3 p(\phi)^3 \sin|\theta - \phi| \, d\theta \, d\phi. \tag{2.73}$$

Using this formula we can evaluate T_1 for any particular case.

2.33 Consider first the triangle. Let AXY be a triangle and suppose that its area is to be increased by moving XY parallel to itself. Then if W is a point on XY distant x from X we must evaluate T when W is the fixed vertex of the random triangle, and then average over all positions of W obtained by taking x to be uniformly distributed on the line XY (Fig. 2.7).

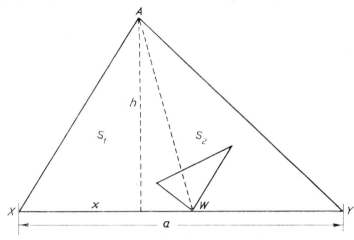

Fig. 2.7

Let S_1 and S_2 be the areas of AXW and AWY and $S(= S_1 + S_2)$ be that of AXY. If $XY = a$ and the height of the triangle is h, we have $S = \frac{1}{2}ah$, $S_1 = \frac{1}{2}xh$, $S_2 = \frac{1}{2}(a-x)h$, and

$$S^2 T = S_1^2 T_{11} + S_2^2 T_{22} + 2S_1 S_2 T_{12}$$

in the previous notation. Substituting the values of the T's we get

$$T = \frac{h}{2a^2}\{\tfrac{4}{27}x^3 + \tfrac{4}{27}(a-x)^3 + \tfrac{2}{9}ax(a-x)\}. \tag{2.74}$$

We then have

$$T_1 = h(2a^2)^{-1} \int_0^a \{\tfrac{4}{27}x^3 + \tfrac{4}{27}(a-x)^3 + \tfrac{2}{9}ax(a-x)\}\,dx \tag{2.75}$$

$$= \tfrac{1}{18}ah = \tfrac{1}{9}S,$$

so that
$$P = 1 - 3T_1 S^{-1} = \tfrac{2}{3} = 0.6667 \tag{2.76}$$

2.34 For a circle we may imagine the enlarged domain to be a concentric circle. All positions of the fixed point on the circumference are then equally likely, and since the figure is circularly symmetric no averaging is necessary. Let a be the radius of the circle. Then $P = 1 - 3T_1(\pi a^2)^{-1}$. A being a point of the circumference, we use it as the origin of polar coordinates, measuring angles from the tangent at A as before. Then

$$T_1 = \frac{32a^2}{9\pi^2} \int_0^\pi \int_0^\pi \sin^3\theta \sin^3\phi \sin|\theta - \phi|\,d\theta\,d\phi$$

$$= \frac{35a^2}{36\pi} \tag{2.77}$$

Then
$$P = 1 - 35\,(12\pi^2)^{-1} = 0{\cdot}7045\dots. \tag{2.78}$$

Deltheil (1926) carries out a similar calculation for a general convex quadrilateral. For the particular case of a parallelogram or rectangle $P = \frac{25}{36} = 0{\cdot}6944$. It can be shown that the value for any convex quadrilateral lies between this value and $0{\cdot}6667$, the value for a triangle. For a regular hexagon $P = 683\,(972)^{-1} = 0{\cdot}7029$ and for an octagon

$$P = \frac{2851 + 2013\sqrt{2}}{4032 + 2880\sqrt{2}} = 0{\cdot}7030. \tag{2.79}$$

Thus for any convex domain P is a characteristic number depending on its shape but not its size. Deltheil proves that for all convex figures P is not less than its value for a triangle and conjectures that for all such figures it is not greater than the value for a circle (or ellipse). This has apparently not yet been proved.

Non-overlapping circles on a plane

2.35 In analogy with the case of random non-overlapping intervals in an interval it would be desirable to define random non-overlapping circles, all of the same size, in a plane. Such a definition has not been obtained and leads to great difficulties, as the following argument shows. Suppose that all the circles have diameter d and one has a centre at a point P. No other circle can have its centre less than $2d$ from P, but the likelihood of such a circle having its centre in a small region of area dS at a distance $R > 2d$ will not be proportional to dS alone and will not in general be a monotonic function of R. This may be seen by considering the limiting case when the density of the circles becomes so large that they are nearly arranged in the manner of "closest packing", i.e. with their centres nearly at the vertices of a lattice of equiangular triangles. The probability of lying in a region dS distant R from a given circle will then be a strongly peaked function of R.

2.36 Another method of approaching this problem, in the case of n non-overlapping circles in a given domain D, would be to suppose that the circles are placed in the domain one after another, all available positions at each stage being taken as equally probable. (This method is similar to that discussed above for intervals on the line.) However, it is then not hard to see that the distributions of the circles are not all the same and depend on their order in the sequence in which they are placed.

Similar difficulties arise in the case of random non-overlapping spheres in space, as will be discussed in a later section.

2.37 When the density of the circles is low no great error will occur if their centres are regarded as points distributed at random on the plane, for the chances of two centres being closer than $2d$ will be small. One interesting application of this occurs in forestry (Bitterlick (p. 148), Grosenbaugh (1952a, 1952b) and Shanks (1954)). Suppose circles, representing tree trunks, are distributed at random sufficiently sparsely for the above approximation to hold and such that the expected number in any area dS is $\lambda\,dS$. Suppose further that the probability distribution of the diameters d of the trunks is $f(d)$. Then the mean area covered by tree trunks is

$$\tfrac{1}{4}\pi\lambda \int_0^\infty x^2 f(x)\,dx. \tag{2.80}$$

Suppose that a random point P is chosen and that the number, N, of trees whose trunks subtend a greater angle than α at P is counted. Such a count can easily be made with a suitable sighting angle and instruments for this purpose have been constructed. A tree will thus be counted if its distance R is such that

$$d > 2R\sin\alpha. \tag{2.81}$$

Hence for a given d in the range $(d, d+dx)$ the average number of such trees counted will be

$$\pi\lambda f(d)\left(\frac{d}{2\sin\alpha}\right)^2, \tag{2.82}$$

and averaging over all values of d, the average number counted will be

$$\frac{\pi\lambda}{4\sin^2\alpha}\int_0^\infty x^2 f(x)\,dx,$$

$$= (\sin^2\alpha)^{-1}\ (\text{mean area of trunks per unit area}). \tag{2.83}$$

In practice α may be chosen to be $1°\,44'$ and then ten times the observed number of trees will give an estimate of square feet of basal area per acre.

Random points in three dimensions

2.38 We now consider random points in three dimensions and suppose again that we have a Poisson field such that the number of points occurring in any region of volume V is a Poisson variate with mean λV. Let P be any fixed point and $r_1, r_2, \ldots$ the distances to the nearest random point, the second nearest random point, and so on. The probability that there is no point in a sphere of radius r about P is

$$\exp-\tfrac{4}{3}\lambda\pi r^3, \tag{2.84}$$

and so the distribution of r_1 is such that $\tfrac{4}{3}\lambda\pi r_1^3$ has a negative exponential distribution, i.e.

$$4\lambda \pi r_1^2 \exp\left\{-\tfrac{4}{3}\lambda \pi r_1^3\right\} dr_1. \tag{2.85}$$

This may also be expressed by saying that $\tfrac{4}{3}\lambda \pi r_1^3$ has the χ^2 distribution with two degrees of freedom. Similarly the distribution of r_s is

$$3\left(\tfrac{4}{3}\lambda \pi\right)^s \Gamma(s)^{-1} \exp-\tfrac{4}{3}\lambda \pi r_s^3 \, r_s^{3s-1} \, dr_s. \tag{2.86}$$

This can be seen directly by observing that the probability of a point occurring in the spherical region $(r, r+dr)$ is $4\lambda \pi r^2 \, dr + o\,(dr)$ and hence

$$\tfrac{4}{3}\lambda \pi r_1^3, \quad \tfrac{4}{3}\lambda \pi \left(r_2^3 - r_1^3\right), \quad \ldots \tag{2.87}$$

are distributed as the intervals to the right of a fixed point on a line on which random points are occurring with unit density.

These distributions have long been known but repeatedly rediscovered (see, for example, Hertz (1909), Pepper (1929)). They have some interesting applications in Astronomy of which we consider two briefly.

Olbers' paradox

2.39 The first of these is Olbers' paradox about the brightness of the night sky (Bondi (1952)). This is a paradox which arises from assuming that there are an infinite number of stars uniformly distributed at random in an infinite space. It is easy to see that the brightness of a star as seen by the eye, divided by the solid angle subtended by the star, is independent of the size and position of the star, provided the latter has a constant brightness at its surface. Suppose for simplicity that all stars have equal diameters δ and the same surface brightness, and let λ be their mean density in unit volume. If a fraction Y of the total solid angle 4π is covered by star disks lying within a distance R from the observing point P, there will be a solid angle $4\pi(1-Y)$ which would be dark if there were no stars beyond R. The expected number of stars in the range $(R, R+dR)$ is $4\lambda \pi R^2 \, dR$ and these subtend a total solid angle at P equal to $\lambda \pi^2 \delta^2 \, dR$, of which a fraction Y will on the average be screened by nearer stars. Hence the increase in the solid angle illuminated due to stars in $(R, R+dR)$ will be $\lambda(1-Y)\pi^2\delta^2 \, dR$, and we have

$$\frac{dY}{dR} = \lambda(1-Y)\pi^2\delta^2 \, dR, \tag{2.88}$$

so that

$$\log(1-Y) = \text{const.} - \lambda(1-Y)\pi^2\delta^2 \, R, \tag{2.89}$$

and hence as $R \to \infty$, $Y \to 1$. This argument applies also to any particular solid angle with vertex at P, and the night sky should therefore be uniformly bright, which is in contradiction with observation.

The reader may easily verify that if there was a uniformly distributed interstellar dust which could act as a screen the above conclusion would not hold. This is not accepted as an explanation since the dust would be expected to reradiate the energy it receives. Bondi gives an extensive discussion of the various physical theories which have been put forward to explain this result.

Holtsmark's problem

2.40 A more difficult problem solved by Holtsmark (1919a, 1919b, 1924)—see also Chandrasekhar (1943a, 1943b, 1944a, 1944b)—is that of the distribution of the gravitational force at a point in space due to a random distribution of stars. If the force is written as a vector $\mathbf{F} = (F_1, F_2, F_3)$ we write this distribution as

$$W(\mathbf{F})\,dF_1\,dF_2\,dF_3. \tag{2.90}$$

Suppose the stars are distributed in the Poisson manner in such a way that the expected number in any volume V has mean λV. If there are N stars in a sphere of radius R about the point O at which the force is to be measured, the force will be

$$\mathbf{F} = G \sum_{i=1}^{N} \frac{M_i}{|r_i|^3} \mathbf{r}_i = \sum_{i=1}^{N} \mathbf{F}_i, \tag{2.91}$$

where M_i is the mass of the ith star and $\mathbf{r}_i = (x_i, y_i, z_i)$ is the vector from 0 to the centre of the star. We obtain the required distribution by letting the N stars take positions randomly distributed throughout the sphere and then letting R and N tend to infinity in such a way that

$$\tfrac{4}{3}\pi R^3 \lambda = N. \tag{2.92}$$

Then if $\mathbf{F}_0$ is the force at O due to the N stars, its distribution will be given by

$$W_N(\mathbf{F}_0)\,dF_1\,dF_2\,dF_3$$
$$= dF_1\,dF_2\,dF_3 \frac{1}{8\pi^3} \int_{-\infty}^{\infty} \int_{-\infty}^{\infty} \int_{-\infty}^{\infty} e^{-i\rho.\mathbf{F}} A_N(\boldsymbol{\rho})\,d\rho_1\,d\rho_2\,d\rho_3, \tag{2.93}$$

where $\boldsymbol{\rho} = (\rho_1, \rho_2, \rho_3)$ is a vector, and $A_N(\boldsymbol{\rho})$ is the characteristic function of the distribution of $\mathbf{F}$. Since $\mathbf{F}$ is the vector sum of the N forces exercised by the N stars, this characteristic function will be the product of the characteristic functions of the distributions of the forces exercised by each of the N stars and will be given by

$$\prod_{i=1}^{N} \int_0^{\infty} dM_i \int\int\int_{|r_i|=0}^{R} e^{i\rho.\mathbf{F}} \tau(M)\,dx_i\,dy_i\,dz_i, \tag{2.94}$$

where we have now averaged over the distribution of the masses of the

G.P.—D

stars, it being assumed that each such mass is independently distributed in a distribution with probability density $\tau(M)$.

We can therefore write $A_N(\boldsymbol{\rho})$ as

$$\left\{\frac{3}{4\pi R^3}\int_0^\infty dM \int\int\int_{|\mathbf{r}|=0}^R e^{i\boldsymbol{\rho}.\boldsymbol{\varphi}}\,\tau(M)\,dx\,dy\,dz\right\}^N, \tag{2.95}$$

where

$$\boldsymbol{\phi} = GM\,\frac{\mathbf{r}}{|\mathbf{r}|^3}. \tag{2.96}$$

Letting R and N tend to infinity we then get

$$W(\mathbf{F}) = \frac{1}{8\pi^3}\int\int\int_{-\infty}^\infty e^{i\boldsymbol{\rho}.\mathbf{F}}A(\boldsymbol{\rho})\,d\rho_1\,d\rho_2\,d\rho_3, \tag{2.97}$$

where

$$A(\boldsymbol{\rho}) = \lim_{R\to\infty}\left\{\frac{3}{4\pi R^3}\int_0^\infty dM \int\int\int_{|\mathbf{r}|=0}^\infty e^{i\boldsymbol{\rho}.\boldsymbol{\varphi}}\tau(M)\,dx\,dy\,dz\right\}^{\frac{4\pi R^3\lambda}{3}}. \tag{2.98}$$

By definition

$$\frac{3}{4\pi R^3}\int_0^\infty dM \int\int\int_{|\mathbf{r}|=0}^R \tau(M)\,dx\,dy\,dz = 1,$$

so that, by subtracting, we can write $A(\boldsymbol{\rho})$ as

$$\lim_{R\to\infty}\left\{1-\frac{3}{4\pi R^3}\int_0^\infty dM \int\int\int_{|\mathbf{r}|=0}^R \tau(M)\{1-e^{i\boldsymbol{\rho}.\boldsymbol{\varphi}}\}\,dx\,dy\,dz\right\}^{\frac{4\pi R^3\lambda}{3}}. \tag{2.99}$$

$\boldsymbol{\phi}$ is $O(|\mathbf{r}|^{-2})$ but since the integral over the sphere is the integral of an odd function of x, y and z, the integrand is effectively $O(|\mathbf{r}|^{-4})$, and hence if the integral is taken over the whole of space it is absolutely convergent. We can therefore write

$$A(\boldsymbol{\rho}) = \lim_{R\to\infty}\left\{1-\frac{3}{4\pi R^3}\int_0^\infty dM \int\int\int_{|\mathbf{r}|=0}^\infty \tau(M)\{1-e^{i\boldsymbol{\rho}.\boldsymbol{\varphi}}\}\,dx\,dy\,dz\right\}^{\frac{4\pi R^3\lambda}{3}}$$

$$= \exp\{-nC(\boldsymbol{\rho})\}, \tag{2.100}$$

where

$$C(\boldsymbol{\rho}) = \int_0^\infty dM \int\int\int_{|\mathbf{r}|=0}^\infty \tau(M)\{1-\exp i\boldsymbol{\rho}.\boldsymbol{\phi}\}\,dx\,dy\,dz. \tag{2.101}$$

Let the vector $\boldsymbol{\phi}$ have components ϕ_1, ϕ_2, ϕ_3 and change the variables of integration in $C(\boldsymbol{\rho})$ from x, y, z to ϕ_1, ϕ_2, ϕ_3. It is not hard to verify by calculation of the Jacobian, that

$$dx\,dy\,dz = -\tfrac{1}{2}(GM)^{\frac{3}{2}}|\boldsymbol{\phi}|^{-\frac{9}{2}}d\phi_1\,d\phi_2\,d\phi_3 \tag{2.102}$$

so that

$$C(\boldsymbol{\rho}) = \tfrac{1}{2}G^{\frac{3}{2}}\int_0^\infty M^{\frac{3}{2}}\tau(M)\,dM \int\int\int_{-\infty}^\infty \{1-\exp i\boldsymbol{\rho}.\boldsymbol{\phi}\}|\boldsymbol{\phi}|^{-\frac{9}{2}}d\phi_1\,d\phi_2\,d\phi_3$$

$$= \tfrac{1}{2} G^2 \mu_{\frac{3}{2}} \iiint_{-\infty}^{\infty} \{1 - \exp i\boldsymbol{\rho}.\boldsymbol{\phi}\} |\boldsymbol{\phi}|^{-\frac{9}{2}} d\phi_1 \, d\phi_2 \, d\phi_3, \qquad (2.103)$$

where $\mu_{\frac{3}{2}}$ is the expected value of $M^{\frac{3}{2}}$. The integrand is unaffected by replacing $\boldsymbol{\phi}$ by $-\boldsymbol{\phi}$, so that we can write it as

$$\tfrac{1}{2} G^2 \mu_{\frac{3}{2}} \iiint_{-\infty}^{\infty} \{1 - \cos \boldsymbol{\rho}.\boldsymbol{\phi}\} |\boldsymbol{\phi}|^{-\frac{9}{2}} d\phi_1 \, d\phi_2 \, d\phi_3. \qquad (2.104)$$

We now transform to three-dimensional polar coordinates, taking the z axis as the direction of $\boldsymbol{\rho}$, and $C(\boldsymbol{\rho})$ becomes

$$\tfrac{1}{2} G^2 \mu_{\frac{3}{2}} |\boldsymbol{\rho}|^{\frac{3}{2}} \int_0^\infty \int_{-1}^1 \int_0^{2\pi} \{1 - \cos(zt)\} z^{-\frac{5}{2}} \, dw \, dt \, dz, \qquad (2.105)$$

where $0 \leqslant w \leqslant 2\pi$, $-1 \leqslant t \leqslant 1$, and $0 \leqslant z < \infty$. Integrating over w and t we get

$$2\pi G^2 \mu_{\frac{3}{2}} |\boldsymbol{\rho}|^{\frac{3}{2}} \int_0^\infty (z - \sin z) z^{-\frac{7}{2}} \, dz = \tfrac{4}{15}(2\pi G)^{\frac{3}{2}} \mu_{\frac{3}{2}} |\boldsymbol{\rho}|^{\frac{3}{2}}. \qquad (2.106)$$

Writing

$$a = \tfrac{4}{15}(2\pi b)^{\frac{3}{2}} \mu_{\frac{3}{2}}, \qquad (2.107)$$

we get

$$W(\mathbf{F}) = \frac{1}{8\pi^2} \iiint_{-\infty}^{\infty} \exp(-i\boldsymbol{\rho}.\mathbf{F} - a|\boldsymbol{\rho}|^{\frac{3}{2}}) \, d\rho_1 \, d\rho_2 \, d\rho_3. \qquad (2.108)$$

To evaluate this we again change to polar coordinates, using the direction of $\mathbf{F}$ as the principal axis, thus obtaining

$$W(\mathbf{F}) = \frac{1}{4\pi^2} \int_0^\infty \int_{-1}^1 \exp(-i|\boldsymbol{\rho}||\mathbf{F}|t - a|\boldsymbol{\rho}|^{\frac{3}{2}}) |\boldsymbol{\rho}|^2 \, dt \, d|\boldsymbol{\rho}|$$

$$= \frac{1}{2\pi^2} \int_0^\infty |\mathbf{F}|^{-1} \exp(-a|\boldsymbol{\rho}|^{\frac{3}{2}}) |\boldsymbol{\rho}| \sin(|\boldsymbol{\rho}||\mathbf{F}|) \, d|\boldsymbol{\rho}|$$

$$= \frac{1}{2\pi |\mathbf{F}|^3} \int_0^\infty \exp(-a x^{\frac{3}{2}} |\mathbf{F}|^{-\frac{3}{2}}) x \sin x \, dx. \qquad (2.109)$$

$a^{\frac{2}{3}}$ has the dimensions of a force, and expressing $\mathbf{F}$ in terms of this as a unit so that $|\mathbf{F}| = \beta a^{\frac{2}{3}}$ the distribution of $|\mathbf{F}|$ becomes

$$W(\mathbf{F}) = H(\beta)/4\pi a^2 \beta^2 \qquad (2.110)$$

where

$$H(\beta) = \frac{2}{\pi \beta} \int_0^\infty \exp\left(-\left(\frac{x}{\beta}\right)^{\frac{3}{2}}\right) x \sin x \, dx. \qquad (2.111)$$

In his (1943) paper Chandrasekhar gives a table of $H(\beta)$ for $\beta = 0\,(0\cdot1)\,3\cdot0\,(0\cdot2)\,3\cdot4\,(1\cdot0)\,4\cdot4\,(0\cdot2)\,10\cdot0\,(5\cdot0)\,50\cdot0\,(10\cdot0)\,100\cdot0$.

2.41 In fact this distribution is not substantially different from the distribution of the force at 0 due to the nearest star alone. Using the previous results this is easily seen to be

$$W(|\mathbf{F}|)\,d\,|\mathbf{F}| = \exp\left(-4\pi\,(GM)^{\frac{3}{2}}\lambda/3\,|\mathbf{F}|^{\frac{3}{2}}\right)2\pi\,(GM)^{\frac{3}{2}}\lambda\,|\mathbf{F}|^{-\frac{5}{2}}d\,|\mathbf{F}|$$

(2.112)

which is easily tabulated. Neither of these distributions can be expected to be very accurate when $\mathbf{F}$ is large since stars have a non-zero volume and their centres cannot therefore approach arbitrarily close to one another.

2.42 The same distributions apply in dealing with the electric field at a point in a gas composed of simple ions. A more difficult question in both these physical problems is to study $\mathbf{F}$ when regarded as the variate of a random process resulting from the random movement of the stars (or ions) in space. This is discussed in great detail in Chandrasekhar and von Neumann (1942, 1943).

Non-overlapping spheres

2.43 In the derivation of the Holtsmark distribution we have assumed that the diameters of the stars are so small compared with the average distance to a nearest neighbour that the assumption of a Poisson distribution gives a good approximation. Here again, as in the case of non-overlapping circles, it does not seem possible to give a simple definition of a random distribution of non-overlapping spheres. Such a definition would be of considerable interest in the theory of liquids (Hildebrand, 1944, Frenkel, 1946).

2.44 Suppose that O is the centre of a sphere and that all spheres have the same diameter d. No other sphere can have its centre at a distance less than $2d$ from O. If the average density of spheres per unit volume is λ and if the effect of the non-zero diameters is ignored, we should expect the average number of spheres whose centres lie at a distance in the interval $(r, r+dr)$ to be $4\lambda\pi r^2\,dr$. The deviation from the ideal state may then be accounted for by introducing a factor $W(r)$, so that the expected number is

$$4\lambda\pi\,W(r)\,r^2\,dr.$$

(2.113)

In practice, this factor can be determined for the distances between molecules in a liquid by X-ray analysis but is very difficult to derive by theoretical methods (e.g. Kirkwood and Boggs, 1942).

2.45 An interesting experimental attempt to determine $W(r)$ in a situation of plausible application was made by Hildebrand and Morrell (1936). A number of gelatine spheres, including a few which were coloured, were placed in a cubic glass vessel containing a gelatine solution of the same density and refractive index. The vessel was repeatedly shaken and photographs taken in two directions at right angles so that the positions of the coloured balls could be measured. In this way an approximate Monte Carlo determination of $W(r)$ was made.

2.46 As the density of the spheres increases, the distribution tends to a discrete distribution which is obtained by considering the set of distances from the centre of one sphere to its near neighbours in the well-known "closest packing" of spheres. This is obtained by arranging spheres in successive layers in each of which their centres form a hexagonal lattice, and such that successive layers lie in the hollows of the layer below. It is a curious fact that although this has been believed for a long time to be the closest packing of spheres no rigorous proof has ever been given.

Distribution of two points in a sphere

2.47 It is easy to invent problems involving a fixed number of points in three-dimensional regions similar to those already discussed above in two dimensions. We consider only one of these, that of the probability distribution of the distance between two points taken at random inside a sphere. It is, however, convenient to consider the more general problem of the distribution of the distance between two points in a hypersphere in n dimensions. This problem is solved in Deltheil (1926) by using Crofton's theorem, and by Hammersley (1950) using direct integration. We follow another method due to Lord (1954) using characteristic functions.

2.48 Let P and Q be the two points in the hypersphere and suppose they are determined by vectors $\mathbf{r}_1$ and $\mathbf{r}_2$. Then we require the distribution of $|\mathbf{r}_1 - \mathbf{r}_2|$ when P and Q are uniformly distributed over the hypersphere and this is the same as the distribution of $|\mathbf{R}|$ where $\mathbf{R} = \mathbf{r}_1 + \mathbf{r}_2$.

Let $\mathbf{r}$ be the vector determining a point which has a uniform distribution in the sphere and write $P(r)\,dr$ for the probability that $r < |\mathbf{r}| < r + dr$. If $\boldsymbol{\rho} = (\rho_1, \rho_2, \rho_3)$ is an arbitrary vector, the characteristic function of $\mathbf{r}$ is

$$E(e^{i\boldsymbol{\rho}\cdot\mathbf{r}}), \qquad (2.114)$$

and for a spherical distribution this is a function of $|\boldsymbol{\rho}|$ only, so that the characteristic function of $r = |\mathbf{r}|$ is

$$\Phi(\rho) = \int_0^\infty P(r)\,\Lambda_{\frac{1}{2}n-1}(r\rho)\,dr, \qquad (2.115)$$

where $\rho = |\boldsymbol{\rho}|$ and

$$\Lambda_\alpha(x) = \Gamma(1+\alpha)(\tfrac{1}{2}x)^{-\alpha}J_\alpha(x). \qquad (2.116)$$

This has an inversion formula

$$P(r) = 2^{1-\frac{1}{2}n}\{\Gamma(\tfrac{1}{2}n)\}^{-1}\int_0^\infty (r\rho)^{\frac{1}{2}n}J_{\frac{1}{2}n-1}(r\rho)\,\Phi(\rho)\,d\rho. \qquad (2.117)$$

Since $J_\alpha(x)$ is a Bessel function, these formulae are Hankel transforms.

For a uniform distribution in a sphere of radius a we have

$$P(r) = nr^{n-1}a^{-n} \quad (0 \leqslant r \leqslant a),$$
$$= 0 \qquad\qquad (r > a). \qquad (2.118)$$

The characteristic function is then

$$\Phi(\rho) = \int_0^\infty nr^{n-1}a^{-n}\Lambda_{\frac{1}{2}n-1}(r\rho)\,dr$$
$$= \Lambda_{\frac{1}{2}n-1}(a\rho). \qquad (2.119)$$

The characteristic function of $|\mathbf{r}| = |\mathbf{r}_1+\mathbf{r}_2|$ is therefore the square of this and

$$P(r) = n\Gamma(1+\tfrac{1}{2}n)\left(\frac{2r}{a^2}\right)^{\frac{1}{2}n}\int_0^\infty \rho^{-\frac{1}{2}n}J_{\frac{1}{2}n}^2(a\rho)J_{\frac{1}{2}n-1}(r\rho)\,d\rho. \qquad (2.120)$$

Substituting in a standard formula (Watson, 1944, p. 411), we find that

$$P(r) = \frac{n\Gamma(\tfrac{1}{2}n+1)}{\Gamma(\tfrac{1}{2}n+\tfrac{1}{2})\Gamma(\tfrac{1}{2})}r^{n-1}a^{-n}\int_A^\pi \cos^2\tfrac{1}{2}\phi\,d\phi, \qquad (2.121)$$

where $0 \leqslant A \leqslant \pi$ and $\sin\tfrac{1}{2}A = \dfrac{r}{2a}$. Put $t = \cos^2\tfrac{1}{2}\phi$ and this becomes

$$P(r) = nr^{k-1}a^{-n}I_\mu(\tfrac{1}{2}n+\tfrac{1}{2}, \tfrac{1}{2}), \qquad (2.122)$$

where $\mu = 1-r^2(4a^2)^{-1}$ and $I_x(p, q)$ is the incomplete Beta function defined by

$$I_x(p, q) = \frac{\Gamma(p+q)}{\Gamma(p)\Gamma(q)}\int_0^x t^{p-1}(1-t)^{q-1}\,dt. \qquad (2.123)$$

If we put $2ay = r$ we get for $n = 1, 2$, and 3,

$$P(r) = 2(1-y), \qquad (2.124)$$

$$P(r) = \frac{16}{\pi}y\{\cos^{-1}-y(1-y^2)^{\frac{1}{2}}\}, \qquad (2.125)$$

and

$$P(r) = 12y^2(1-y)^2(2+y), \qquad (2.126)$$

which correspond to the cases for a segment, a circle, and a three-dimensional sphere. In particular (2.125) is another way of writing the previously obtained result for a circle.

2.49 From this we can obtain the moments, and the rth moment of $P Q$ in a sphere of radius a in a space of n dimensions is

$$\frac{n\Gamma(n+1)\Gamma(\tfrac{1}{2}n+\tfrac{1}{2}r+\tfrac{1}{2})(2a)^r}{\Gamma(\tfrac{1}{2}n+\tfrac{1}{2})(n+r)\Gamma(n+\tfrac{1}{2}r+1)}. \tag{2.127}$$

When n becomes large it can be shown that the distribution of $P Q$ tends to normality with mean $a2^{\frac{1}{2}}$ and variance $a^2(2n)^{-1}$. For other work on the problem see Watson (1959).

Clearly this problem can be extended to other domains, and in the case of a cylinder the results have practical applications (see Hammersley, 1951a, 1951b, 1952).

The distribution of the distance between points constrained to lie on the surface of a sphere could be considered in the same way.

CHAPTER 3

RANDOM LINES IN A PLANE AND IN SPACE

Regions determined by random lines in a plane

3.1 We have already seen in Chapter 1 that the most natural coordinates to use for the description of lines in a plane are (p, θ), the polar

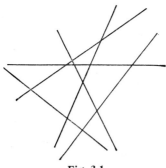

coordinates of the foot of the perpendicular from the origin on to the line. With this representation the area element in the parameter space which is invariant under Euclidean transformations is $dp\, d\theta$. Hence we suppose that such lines are distributed "at random" in the sense that we have a Poisson field with density $\lambda dp\, d\theta$. The lines from a field of this type will divide the plane into an infinite number of polygonal regions, as in Fig. 3.1.

Fig. 3.1

3.2 The probability distribution of the areas of such regions is of very great interest, but its analytical form is not known exactly. Some facts about it are, however, known (Goudsmit, 1945). One method of approach would be to consider the intersections of a large number of random chords of a circle, but a more elegant method, due to Goudsmit, is to consider this as the limit of another problem, namely that of the distribution of the areas of the regions on the surface of a sphere which are formed by a large number of random "great circles", i.e. circles formed by the intersections with planes through the centre of the sphere. Such a circle can be defined by the coordinates of one of its "poles" on the surface of the sphere, and we can then suppose that each of these poles is uniformly distributed over the surface of the sphere.

3.3 Suppose the sphere has unit radius, and let n be the number of great circles. For n equal to 1 the number of distinct regions is 2, for $n = 2$ it is 4, for $n = 3$ it is 8, and by induction it is easily seen that in general the number of areas is $2 + n(n-1)$ since when n is changed into $n+1$, $2n$ new regions are added. Similarly for $n = 2, 3, 4$ the number of sides (taken as equal to the number of segments of the great circles) is 4, 12, and 24 respectively, whilst for general n it is $2n(n-1)$. Thus, as n becomes large the average area is asymptotically equal to $4\pi n^{-2}$, whilst the average number of sides of each quasi-polygonal region will be the limit of

$$\frac{4n(n-1)}{2+n(n-1)}$$

which is 4. (The numerator is here $4n(n-1)$ and not $2n(n-1)$ since each segment of a great circle is a side to two polygonal areas and must be counted twice.) The total perimeter of the $2+n(n-1)$ regions is twice the total length of all the great circles, i.e. it is $4\pi n$, so that the average perimeter of a region is asymptotically equal to $4\pi n^{-1}$, and the average length of each side is πn^{-1}.

3.4 We now suppose that n becomes very large and consider the distribution of regions in a small circle of radius r on the surface of the sphere. The number of great circles which intersect this small circle will be asymptotically equal to rn. Proceeding to the limit and considering the region inside this small circle as approximately a plane circle, we find, on rescaling, that the average area of the regions in a plane formed by a Poisson field with density $\lambda dp\,d\theta$ is $(\pi\lambda^2)^{-1}$. In an unpublished paper Mr. D. G. Kendall has also found the second moment of the area, but the exact distribution is still unknown. A similar investigation could also be made for the regions formed by random planes in space, as we shall see in the next chapter.

Convex figures in a plane

3.5 A large number of interesting problems in geometrical probability are connected with convex figures. For the most part they involve a fixed number of intersecting random lines, usually one or two. The resulting theories are closely related to the large subject of convex figures in general, of which a detailed account has been given by Bonnesen and Fenchel (1948) which covers the literature to 1933 (for subsequent work see Hadwiger, 1955).

The theory of convex figures in geometrical probability is mainly due to Barbier (1860), Crofton (1869, 1877, 1885) and Sylvester (1891).

3.6 A convex figure in a plane is a set of points, usually closed, which is such that if P_1 and P_2 are any two points in it, so also are all the points of the interval P_1P_2. If the set is bounded, its boundary is a closed curve with a tangent almost everywhere. It may be defined by the pair of periodic functions $\{x(t), y(t)\}$ $(0 \leqslant t \leqslant 1$, say) giving the coordinates of a point on the boundary where $x(1) = x(0), y(1) = y(0)$. In many circumstances it is more convenient to define it by giving its "function of support" with reference to an origin O. This function, $H(\theta)$, may be defined as the distance (Fig. 3.2) of O from the tangent perpendicular

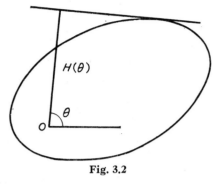

Fig. 3.2

to a line radiating from the point O in the direction θ, i.e. the length of the pedal in terms of θ. O is usually taken inside the convex figure, but if outside only a slight variation of the definition is necessary. Then $H(\theta)$ is a periodic function of θ with period 2π, and the function $H(\theta) + H(\pi + \theta)$ is the length of the interval which is the projection of the convex figure on any line in the direction θ. This length may be described as the "thickness" of the figure in the direction θ.

3.7 Since we have taken $\lambda dp\, d\theta$ $(p \geqslant 0, 0 \leqslant \theta \leqslant 2\pi)$ as the element of measure in the set of all lines in a plane, the measure of the set of all lines intersecting a convex figure C will be

$$\lambda \int_0^\pi \{H(\theta) + H(\theta + \pi)\}\, d\theta = \lambda \int_0^{2\pi} H(\theta)\, d\theta. \tag{3.1}$$

We shall show that in fact this is equal to λL, the length of contour of C. This follows at once when we observe that when θ increases to $\theta + d\theta$. the corresponding element of length is $dL = H(\theta)\, d\theta$. Thus we can write

$$\iint_C dp\, d\theta = L, \tag{3.2}$$

where the integral is taken over the region in (p, θ) space for which the line cuts the figure. It immediately follows from this that if a convex figure C_2 of length L_2 is contained in a convex figure C_1 of length L_1, the probability that a random chord of C_1 cuts C_2 is $L_2 L_1^{-1}$. Notice that this probability is independent of the position of C_2 relative to C_1. Furthermore we may suppose C_2 to consist of a straight segment of length l. This can be regarded as the limit of a convex region of perimeter converging to $2l$. The probability that a random chord of C_1 intersects this segment is then $2l L_1^{-1}$.

3.8 This can be looked at from another point of view. Consider a straight segment of length l in the plane and its projection on a line in a direction making an angle θ with it. This is $P(\theta) = l|\cos\theta|$ and the mean value of $P(\theta)$ is

$$\frac{1}{2\pi} \int_0^{2\pi} l \, |\cos\theta| \, d\theta = \frac{2l}{\pi}. \tag{3.3}$$

This formula was originally due to Cauchy and has been used by Steinhaus (1930) as the basis of a method for measuring the length of a curve observed under a microscope.

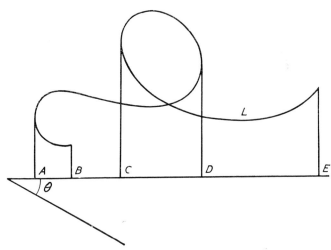

Fig. 3.3

Suppose (Fig. 3.3) that the curve L has length L and that its total projection on a line in the direction θ is measured so that each subinterval of projection is counted as many times as there are points on the curve which project on to it. Thus, in the case shown in the figure, the projection would be taken as

$$P(\theta) = 2AB + BC + 3CD + DE.$$

Then, adding the contributions of each small element of the curve, we see that

$$L = \frac{\pi}{2} \bar{P}, \tag{3.4}$$

where $\bar{P}$ is the mean of $P(\theta)$ taken over all directions. For any given direction $\bar{P}(\theta)$ is easily found if the microscope has a calibrated moving stage. To find P such measurements could be taken with n values of θ spaced $2\pi n^{-1}$ apart. When n is odd this is the same as taking the mean of $2n$ observations spaced πn^{-1} apart, so we consider only the case where $2n$ observations are taken $2\pi (2n)^{-1}$ apart. An exact upper bound for the error is then easily obtained by using elementary vector analysis, for if $\bar{P}_{2n}$ is the mean based on $2n$ observations,

$$\pi\cos\frac{\pi}{2n}\left(2n\sin\frac{\pi}{2n}\right)^{-1} \leqslant \bar{P}_{2n}\bar{P}^{-1} \leqslant \pi\left(2n\sin\frac{\pi}{2n}\right)^{-1}. \qquad (3.5)$$

Even for small n, the resulting error is small.

3.9 Instead of supposing that the figure C_2 lies inside C_1 suppose that it lies entirely outside C_1. We determine again the probability that a random chord of C_1 intersects C_2. Draw the four common tangents AB, CD, EG and FH, the latter two intersecting between the contours in a point O (Fig. 3.4). Define the convex figures Γ_1 and Γ_2 to consist

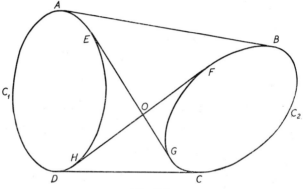

Fig. 3.4

of the figures C_1 and C_2 together with regions interior to the two tangents from O to each, so that Γ_1 is $AEOHD$ and Γ_2 is $BFOGC$. Let L_{12} and L'_{12} be the lengths of chords tightly drawn about C_1 and C_2 and either not crossing over, or crossing over at O. Then we can write

(Measure of chords of Γ_1)+(Measure of chords of Γ_2) = (Measure of all lines which meet either Γ_1 or Γ_2)+(Measure of all lines which meet both Γ_1 and Γ_2.) (3.6)

The left-hand side of this equation is equal, from what has been said before, to the sum of the perimeters of Γ_1 and Γ_2, i.e. to L'_{12} (taking $\lambda = 1$). The measure of the lines which meet either Γ_1 or Γ_2 or both is L_{12}. Thus the measure of the lines which meet both is $L'_{12}-L_{12}$, and since the measure of all chords which meet C_1 is its perimeter L_1 the required probability is

$$(L'_{12}-L_{12})L_1^{-1}. \qquad (3.7)$$

3.10 Similarly we may consider two convex figures which overlap. The number of intersections of the two boundaries may be any even number, but by applying the above type of argument we can see that the probability that a random chord of C_1 intersects C_2 is

$$(L_1 + L_2 - L_{12}) L_1^{-1}, \qquad (3.8)$$

where L_1 and L_2 are the perimeters of C_1 and C_2 and L_{12} is the length of a chord tightly drawn about both, i.e. the length of the "smallest convex cover" of both C_1 and C_2.

3.11 Now consider pairs of lines intersecting a convex figure C of length L. Since the measure of each is L and they are taken as independent the appropriate measure† is L^2. To obtain the probability that two random chords of C will intersect inside C we must find the measure of all pairs of lines which satisfy this condition. More generally, consider another convex figure C_1 contained in C (and possibly identical with it) and determine the probability that two random chords of C_1 intersect inside C_2. Let AB be a chord of C_1 which intersects C_2 and consider the measure of the set of chords of C_1 which intersect AB inside C_2. If x is the length of the intercept of AB by C_2 the measure will be $2x$, and the probability that a random chord of C_1 will intersect this intercept is $2xL_1^{-1}$. If (p, θ) are the coordinates of the line making the chord AB the probability element associated with this line is $L_1^{-1} dp\, d\theta$, and hence the overall probability that the two chords intersect is

$$P = \tfrac{1}{2} \int\int 2x L_1^{-2}\, dp\, d\theta \quad (-\infty < p < \infty, 0 \leqslant \theta \leqslant 2\pi), \quad (3.9)$$

where the integral is taken over all positive and negative values of p and all values of θ, such that the line intersects C_2. Integrating first with respect to p, we see that

$$\int_{-\infty}^{\infty} x\, dp = A_2, \text{ the area of } C_2. \qquad (3.10)$$

Thus

$$P = 2\pi A_2 L_1^{-2}. \qquad (3.11)$$

As a special case we may assume C_1 and C_2 coincide, so that

$$P = 2\pi A_1 L_1^{-2}, \qquad (3.12)$$

and for a circle P is equal to $\tfrac{1}{2}$.

Since $P \leqslant 1$ we have $2\pi A_1 < L_1^2$. This is reminiscent of the classical isoperimetric inequality which states that for any closed non-overlapping curve with A as its internal area and L as the length of its perimeter,

$$4\pi A < L^2. \qquad (3.13)$$

† Deltheil takes $\tfrac{1}{2}L^2$ since he does not give different identities to the two lines, but it is a little clearer to distinguish them and hence each configuration of two lines is counted twice.

From this it follows that the probability of intersection of two random chords of a convex figure never exceeds $\frac{1}{2}$, the value for a circle.

3.12   The other interesting thing about (3.11) is that it shows that the probability depends only on the area of C_2 and not on its position or shape. Hence if we have a large number of random chords of C_1 their intersections will be uniformly spread over the figure with a "density" 2π.

3.13   (3.11) can also be used to give another proof of Goudsmit's result. Take a circle of unit radius for simplicity and suppose it has n random chords. If we add another chord the expected number of intersections is $\frac{1}{2}n$. If we count as regions all those areas which have part of the circumference for a boundary, the number of new areas resulting when there are N intersections is $N+1$, and hence the total expected number of areas with n random chords is

$$1+\tfrac{2}{2}+\tfrac{3}{2}+\ldots+\frac{n+1}{2} = \tfrac{1}{2}+\tfrac{1}{4}(n+1)(n+2). \tag{3.14}$$

The number with curved boundaries is $O(n)$ and hence it does not matter whether we count them or not. The asymptotic number of areas is $\frac{1}{4}n^2$, and from this we deduce the result obtained before to the effect that a Poisson field of lines with density element $\lambda dp\, d\theta$ divides the plane into regions of average area $(\pi\lambda^2)^{-1}$.

Crofton's theorem on convex figures

3.14   We next consider the density of the intersections of chords of a convex figure outside the figure. We do this by determining the probability that two random chords of C_1 will intersect inside a convex figure C_2 (outside C_1) which is such that its area and dimensions are small (Fig. 3.5).

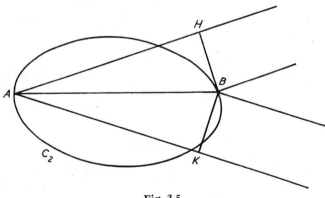

Fig. 3.5

Let AB be the intersection with C_2 of a chord of C_1. From A and B draw tangents of C_1. Then from (3.7) the measure of all chords of C_1 which also intersect AB is the difference between the lengths of chords drawn about C_1 and AB, either crossing or not. Since C_2 is vanishingly small, the tangents from A and B are parallel in pairs. Let BK and BH be the perpendiculars from B on the tangents through A. The required measure is then $2AB-AH-AK$. Let $\theta, \theta_1, \theta_2$ be the directions of AB, AK and AH so that

$$2AB-AH-AK = AB[2-\cos(\theta-\theta_1)-\cos(\theta-\theta_2)].$$

Integrating over all possible values of the parameters defining the line AB, we get

$$\int_{\theta_1}^{\theta_2}\int AB\{2-\cos(\theta-\theta_1)-\cos(\theta-\theta_2)\}\,dp\,d\theta. \tag{3.15}$$

Integrating over p we get

$$\int AB\,dp = \text{area } C_2, \tag{3.16}$$

so that the "density" of intersections of pairs of chords of C_1 is

$$\delta = \int_{\theta_1}^{\theta_2}\{2-\cos(\theta-\theta_1)-\cos(\theta-\theta_2)\}\,d\theta$$
$$= 2\{(\theta_1-\theta_2)-\sin(\theta_1-\theta_2)\}. \tag{3.17}$$

The measure of all pairs of chords of C_1 which intersect in a region D outside C_1 is therefore given by

$$2\int_D\int(\alpha-\sin\alpha)\,dx\,dy, \tag{3.18}$$

where α is the angle subtended by C_1 at the point (x,y). In this formula D could be taken as the whole of the plane outside C_1. Since the measure of all chords of C_1 is L^2, we have

$$2\iint_{\Omega-C_1}(\alpha-\sin\alpha)\,dx\,dy = L^2-2\pi\delta \geqslant 0, \tag{3.19}$$

where Ω is the whole plane. This is Crofton's "first" theorem on convex figures.

3.15 Lebesgue (1912) has given an alternative derivation of (3.19). Consider straight lines l and l' which are possibly restricted to lie in certain sets of lines E and E', and suppose that their equations are written

$$(l) \quad x\cos\theta+y\sin\theta = p,$$
$$(l') \quad x\cos\theta'+y\sin\theta' = p'.$$

Then the measure of their points of intersection is

$$\int\int_E\int\int_{E'} dp\, d\theta\, dp'\, d\theta'.$$

Keeping θ and θ' constant, we can regard p and p' as functions of (x,y), the coordinates of the intersection of l and l'. The Jacobian of the transformation is

$$\left|\frac{\partial(p,p')}{\partial(x,y)}\right| = \left|\begin{matrix}\cos\theta & \sin\theta \\ \cos\theta' & \sin\theta'\end{matrix}\right|$$
$$= |\sin(\theta'-\theta)|,$$

and the integral becomes

$$\int\int\left\{\int\int |\sin(\theta'-\theta)|\,d\theta\, d\theta'\right\} dx\, dy,$$

so that the "density" of the intersections at the point (x,y) is the integral

$$\int\int |\sin(\theta'-\theta)|\,d\theta\, d\theta'$$

taken over the corresponding domain of values of θ and θ'. When the sets E and E' consist of lines intersecting the convex domain C_1, θ and θ' will both vary over a range θ_0 to $\theta_0+\alpha$. Since the integral is independent of θ_0 we can take the latter as zero and obtain

$$\int_0^\alpha d\theta'\left\{\int_0^{\theta'} \sin(\theta'-\theta)\,d\theta - \int_{\theta'}^\alpha \sin(\theta'-\theta)\,d\theta\right\}$$
$$= \int_0^\alpha \{1-\cos\theta'-\cos(\alpha-\theta')+1\}\,d\theta'$$
$$= 2\alpha-2\sin\theta,$$

as before.

3.16 In Lebesgue's method of proving Crofton's "first" theorem of convex figures a measure was set up for pairs of lines in the plane. The same type of method can be used for pairs of points. Suppose we have two points P and P' with coordinates (x,y) and (x',y') restricted to lie in two sets E and E' (which may be the same). Then the natural measure of pairs (P,P') will be

$$\int\int_E\int\int_{E'} dx\, dy\, dx'\, dy'. \tag{3.20}$$

Let $$x\cos\theta + y\sin\theta = p$$
and $$x\sin\theta - y\cos\theta = 0$$

be the equations of the lines PP' and the perpendicular on PP' from the origin of coordinates. If (ξ,η) is a point of the plane, its distance from the line $x\sin\theta - y\cos\theta = 0$ is given by $\xi\sin\theta - \eta\cos\theta$ with a suitable convention as to the sign of this distance. Hence we can replace the set of coordinates (x, y, x', y') of the pair P, P' by the four coordinates (p, θ, ρ, ρ'), where

$$x = \rho \sin \theta + p \cos \theta,$$
$$y = -\rho \cos \theta + p \sin \theta,$$
$$x' = \rho' \sin \theta + p \cos \theta,$$
$$y' = -\rho' \cos \theta + p \sin \theta,$$

and the Jacobian is easily found to be $\rho' - \rho$. Thus the above integral becomes

$$\iiiint |\rho' - \rho| \, d\rho \, d\rho' \, dp \, d\theta, \tag{3.21}$$

and the corresponding range of integration is often simpler than the original one.

Crofton's second theorem on convex figures

3.17 To illustrate this, suppose that C is a convex figure of area A. Then the measure of all pairs of points inside the figure is A^2, each pair, in the geometrical sense, being counted twice. If AB is a chord, the relative density of pairs of points on this chord will be given by

$$\iint |\rho' - \rho| \, d\rho \, d\rho', \tag{3.22}$$

where the pairs have corresponding coordinate value (ρ, ρ'). If a and b are the values of these corresponding to A and B the integral is easily verified to be equal to $\frac{1}{3} l_{AB}^3$, where l_{AB} is the length AB. Thus the integral representing the measure of all pairs of points in C can be written

$$\tfrac{1}{3} \iint l_{AB}^3 \, dp \, d\theta, \tag{3.23}$$

where l_{AB} is the length of the chord intercepted by the line whose polar coordinates are (p, θ). We have already shown that this measure is equal to S^2, and so we obtain the equation

$$\iint l_{AB}^3 \, dp \, d\theta = 3S^2, \tag{3.24}$$

which is Crofton's "second" theorem. Notice in particular that the dimensionality of the formula is correct, both sides being of the fourth order in length.

3.18 This result is easily generalized to obtain the mean of the nth power of the distance apart of two points chosen at random in a convex contour. Proceeding as before, this mean value is

$$A^{-2} \int \int \left\{ \int \int |\rho' - \rho|^{n+1} d\rho \, d\rho' \right\} dp \, d\theta$$

$$= A^{-2} \int \int \left[\int_0^{l_{AB}} d\rho' \left\{ \int_0^{\rho'} |\rho' - \rho|^{n+1} d\rho + \int_{\rho'}^{l_{AB}} |\rho' - \rho|^{n+1} d\rho \right\} \right] dp \, d\theta$$

$$= A^{-2} \int \int \frac{2}{(n+2)(n+3)} l_{AB}^{n+3} \, dp \, d\theta. \tag{3.25}$$

For a circle the mean distance between two points is thus

$$\frac{1}{6\pi^2 R^4} \int_0^{2\pi} d\theta \int_0^R 16 \, (R^2 - p^2)^2 \, dp \; = \; \frac{128R}{45\pi}, \tag{3.26}$$

as obtained before (Chapter 2). In a similar way we could obtain the characteristic function of the distribution of the distance of two points.

3.19 Crofton has given other theorems (1877) on mean values of which the following is typical. Consider a convex figure C which has a centre O, i.e. relative to this centre $H(\theta) = H(\theta + \pi)$, and every chord through O is bisected at O. Let θ be the direction of such a chord and G the centre of gravity of one of the two halves into which the figure is divided by the chord. Then we shall show that the mean distance of points in the figure from O is one-quarter the length of the curve traced out by G as θ increases from zero to 2π.

Let XY be the chord through O and suppose that $\bar{x}, \bar{y}$ are the co-ordinates of G referred to OY as x-axis. If XOY is rotated through a small angle θ to a new position $X'OY'$ it is clear that the new position of G, relative to the old axes, is given by

$$\bar{x}' = \bar{x} + d\bar{x} = A^{-1}\{A\bar{x} + \tfrac{2}{3}aw + \tfrac{2}{3}aw\}, \tag{3.27}$$

where A is the area of the half-figure, a is the distance $OX = OY$, and w is the "weight" associated with the regions XOX' and YOY'. Clearly

$$w = \tfrac{1}{2}a^2 \, d\theta,$$

and

$$A = \int_0^\pi \tfrac{1}{2}a^2 \, d\theta.$$

Similarly $$y' = \bar{y} + d\bar{y} = \bar{y}.$$

Thus G is displaced parallel to XOY, and if we denote an element of its path length by ds we have

$$ds = d\bar{x} = \tfrac{2}{3}a^3 A^{-1} d\theta,$$

so that the radius of curvature of this path is

$$\frac{ds}{d\theta} = \tfrac{2}{3}a^3 A^{-1} = \tfrac{1}{6}l(\theta)^3 A^{-1},$$

where $l(\theta)$ is the length $XY = 2a$. Then the length of the path traced out by G is

$$M = \int ds = (6A)^{-1} \int l(\theta)^3 \, d\theta, \qquad (3.28)$$

whilst the mean distance of points in the figure from O is

$$A^{-1} \int \tfrac{1}{3} a^3 (\theta) \, d\theta = \tfrac{1}{4} M. \qquad (3.29)$$

This result can also be proved by calculating, in two ways, the probability that a random chord and a random point in the figure are such that the centre of the figure and the random point lie on opposite sides of the chord.

Applications in ecology

3.20   The theory of the intersection of random lines with convex or other figures has been applied by G. A. McIntyre (1953) to the estimation of plant cover or areal density in ecology. The figures may be of general shape, or convex, or circles, and the stronger the assumptions which can be legitimately made about them the stronger the conclusions that can be drawn. The method used is to place a straight line, of length L, called a "transect", at random on the area to be surveyed and to measure its intersections with the regions which might, for example, be patches of some particular type of vegetation.

Suppose first that the regions to be estimated are of any shape and that, on the average, they occupy a fraction P of the total area which we shall take as so large that edge effects can be neglected. The regions, which are non-overlapping, are not necessarily distributed "at random" in any sense. Suppose that they intersect the transect in intervals of lengths l_i $(i = 1, 2, ...)$. Then $L^{-1}\Sigma l_i$ is an unbiassed estimator of P. For consider any element dx of the transect. The probability that this lies inside some region is P, and since the expectation of the sum of a set of quantities is the sum of the expectations, the expectation of the sum Σl_i will be LP. An estimate of the variance of the estimate can be obtained by repeating the process a number of times and calculating the sample variance.

3.21   What is of more interest is to be able to estimate the number of regions per unit area in the total area, and it is clear that this cannot be done without making further assumptions about the shape of the regions. We shall suppose them to be circles whose diameters $2R$ have a frequency distribution $\phi(2R)$ and are such that the expected number of circles with diameters in the range $(2R, 2(R+dR))$ which lie in a large area A is

$$2\lambda A\phi(2R)\,dR, \tag{3.30}$$

so that the expected total number of circles in A is λA.

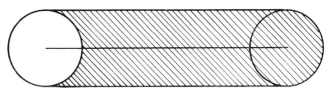

Fig. 3.6

3.22   The transect will form a chord or part chord with any circle which it intersects. We shall first suppose that we count only those intersections with the transect which are whole chords, together with any part chords at one specified end of the transect. Let the resulting intervals be denoted by $l_1', l_2' \ldots$. Then circles of diameter D giving rise to intervals counted in this manner must lie in a region of the type shaded in Fig. 3.6 which has area $2RL$.

The probability that the transect intersects a given circle will be larger if the circle is large and therefore the probability distribution of $2R$ for circles which intersect the transect will be different from $2\phi(2R)\,dR$. In fact the expected number of intersections of the transect with circles whose diameters lie in the range $2R, 2(R+dR)$ will be

$$4LR\lambda\phi(2R)\,dR \tag{3.31}$$

which we shall write as $2f(2R)\,dR$. This is not a probability but is proportional to one, the factor of proportionality being obtained by integration, so that we get

$$\frac{f(2R)\,dR}{\displaystyle\int_0^\infty f(2R)\,dR} = \frac{R\phi(2R)\,dR}{\displaystyle\int R\phi(2R)\,dR} \tag{3.32}$$

as this probability distribution.

3.23   It is now convenient to modify again the rule for counting intersects. We now count all complete chords but omit part chords from one specified end of the transect, and complete any part chords at the other end. Denote the resulting set of intervals by $l_1'', l_2'' \ldots$. Then the expectation of $\Sigma\, l_i''$ is

$$E(\Sigma\, l_i'') = 2\lambda\pi L\int_0^\infty R^2\,\phi(2R)\,dR$$

$$= \pi\int_0^\infty Rf(2R)\,dR, \tag{3.33}$$

because the average length of intersection with a circle of radius R is $\frac{1}{2}\pi R$. We do not know $\phi(2R)$ or $f(2R)$ but the last expression can be written as

$$\frac{\lambda\pi L \int_0^\infty Rf(2R)\,dR}{\int_0^\infty f(2R)\,dR}\left\{\frac{\int_0^\infty R^{-1}f(2R)\,dR}{\int_0^\infty f(2R)\,dR}\right\}^{-1} \tag{3.34}$$

because

$$\int^\infty R^{-1}f(2R)\,dR = 2L\lambda\int_0^\infty \phi(2R)\,dR = L\lambda. \tag{3.35}$$

Hence

$$E(l_i'') = \lambda\pi L E_f(R)\{E_f(R^{-1})\}^{-1}, \tag{3.36}$$

where E_f means the expectation relative to the distribution of diameters of circles which do intersect the transect. We can estimate $E_f(R)$ and $E_f(R^{-1})$ by

$$N^{-1}\Sigma D_i \quad \text{and} \quad N^{-1}\Sigma D_i^{-1}, \tag{3.37}$$

where N is the number of intersections with the transect, and $D_1, D_2, \ldots$ are the (measured) diameters of the circles making the intersections $l_1'', l_2'', \ldots$. Thus an estimate, by no means unbiassed, of λ will be given by the expression

$$(\Sigma l_i'')(\Sigma D_i^{-1})\{\tfrac{1}{4}\pi L \Sigma D_i\}^{-1}. \tag{3.38}$$

3.24 We can in fact replace this by an even simpler estimate using only the values of the intercepts l_i''. For if a line intersects a circle of radius R the probability distribution of the length of intercept l is clearly given by

$$\frac{l\,dl}{2R(4R^2-l^2)^{\frac{1}{2}}}. \tag{3.39}$$

From this we have

$$E(l_i^{-1}) = \tfrac{1}{4}\pi R^{-1}, \tag{3.40}$$

$$E(l_i) = \tfrac{1}{2}\pi R. \tag{3.41}$$

Hence we can replace the above estimator by

$$\frac{(\Sigma l_i'')}{L}\cdot\frac{2\pi^{-1}\Sigma(l_i'')^{-1}}{\Sigma l_i''} = 2\pi^{-1}L^{-1}\Sigma(l_i'')^{-1}. \tag{3.42}$$

These estimators are dependent on the assumption that the regions are circular. In particular, any estimator based on expressions such as $\Sigma(l_i'')^{-1}$ will fail for regions having angles. Various modifications of these techniques are considered by McIntyre for dealing with regions which do not depart too widely from circles.

3.25 We may also point out that it is possible to extend this theory to the estimation of the probability distribution $2\phi(2R)\,dR$ from the frequency distribution of the l_i'', and we shall consider this type of problem in detail in the next chapter in connection with the estimation of the probability distribution of the radii of sets of spheres in three-dimensional spaces from the observed diameters of their intersections with random planes.

Buffon's problem

3.26 We may end our discussion of random lines in a plane by considering the classical problem which was the beginning of this theory—that of Buffon's needle (Buffon, 1777).

A needle length L is placed at random on a plane on which are ruled parallel lines at unit distance apart and the probability is required that the needle intersects these lines. Suppose first that $L < 1$ so that only one intersection is possible. Let θ be the angle made by the needle with the direction of lines, and x the distance of its centre from one of them. Then for x uniformly distributed over the range $(-\frac{1}{2}, \frac{1}{2})$, and θ uniformly distributed over $(0, 2\pi)$, the probability is

$$P = (2\pi)^{-1} \int_0^{2\pi} L\,|\sin\theta|\,d\theta = 2\pi^{-1}L. \qquad (3.43)$$

If L is greater than unity consider the probability of at least one intersection. This is

$$P = \frac{1}{\pi} \int_0^{\sin^{-1} L^{-1}} \{1 - L\,|\sin\theta\,|\}\,d\theta$$

$$= \frac{2}{\pi}\left\{\frac{\pi}{2} - \sin^{-1}L^{-1} + L - \sqrt{(L^2-1)}\right\} \qquad (3.44)$$

If the needle is thrown N times and in R of these throws at least one intersection is obtained, $\hat{P} = RN^{-1}$ is an unbiassed estimator of P with

Table 3.1

Experimenter	Needle length	Throws	Hits	Estimate
Wolf, 1850	0·8	5000	2532	3·1596
Smith, 1855	0·6	3204	1218·5	3·1553
De Morgan, c. 1860	1·0	600	382·5	3·137
Fox, 1884	0·75	1030	489	3·1595
Lazzerini, 1901	0·83	3408	1808	3·1415929
Reina, 1925	0·5419	2520	859	3·1795
Gridgeman, c. 1960	0·7857	2	1	3·143

variance $N^{-1}P(1-P)$. Hence it is possible to estimate π by experiments of this kind. Many such experiments have been made and are summarized and discussed by Gridgeman (1960) in a very interesting paper. Table 3.1 gives some details of these, the needle length being given as a fraction of the interlinear distance.

3.27 The excellent results of these experiments are mainly due to an adroit use of "optional stopping", combined, in Lazzerini's case, with the good fortune that the estimate of π came to $355(113)^{-1}$, a well-known approximation to π discovered by Tsu Ch'ung-chih. If the true value of π was unknown before the experiment, so that optional stopping could not be used, a better method of estimating π is to cut out a large circle of wood and use a tape measure.

3.28 Buffon's problem can be looked at in various ways and several extensions have been considered, some of which throw light on a variety of other probability problems. For instance, suppose that a figure consisting of a line of length L, twisted into a definite shape, is thrown on a set of parallel lines, unit distance apart. Then the expected number of intersections is $2\pi^{-1}l$, independently of the shape. This is really (3.4) looked at in another way.

3.29 Buffon's problem can also be treated (for $L < 1$) by using the previous results on convex figures. For suppose the needle is surrounded by a circle of unit diameter whose centre is the mid-point of the needle. This circle will intersect the lines in exactly one line whose intersection will be a random chord of the circle. From what has been proved before (3.1) it follows that the probability that this chord intersects the needle is $2L/\pi$.

3.30 Although π is naturally best found by quite other methods than an experimental realization of Buffon's problems, such Monte Carlo methods are often necessary in other problems, and to illustrate the important technique of "antithetic variates" Hammersley and Morton (1956) discuss a variation which is of great interest in suggesting similar methods in other applications.

3.31 Suppose that the needle has unit length, and, in order to simplify the algebra, let the distance between the parallel lines be so small that a count of the number of intersections is equivalent to measuring the length of the projection of the needle in a direction parallel to the parallel lines. Thus each observation is a random variable $X = |\sin\theta|$, where

θ is uniformly distributed on $(0, 2\pi)$. Then X is an unbiassed estimator of $2\pi^{-1}$ with a coefficient of variation equal to $\sqrt{(\frac{1}{8}\pi^2 - 1)} = 0 \cdot 4834$.

3.32 If T is a variate used as an estimator in a Monte Carlo method, an antithetic variate T' is one with the same expectation as T and which is dependent on T in such a way that T' is large when T is small and vice versa. Adding the two together, we may hope for a much improved estimate. Hammersley and Morton illustrate this principle by considering the projection of another similar needle fixed at right angles to the first. We then have

$$X' = \tfrac{1}{2}\{|\sin\theta| + |\cos\theta|\} \qquad (3.45)$$

as an unbiassed estimator of $2\pi^{-1}$ with a coefficient of variation which can be verified to be equal to $\sqrt{\{\frac{1}{16}\pi^2 + \frac{1}{8}\pi - 1\}} = 0 \cdot 0977$. Thus even if there is twice as much labour in each throw in the second method, the efficiency is $12 \cdot 2$ times the first method. This idea can be further extended by using n needles in the form of a star with angles πn^{-1} between successive needles. The coefficient of variation of the mean projection can then be shown to be

$$\pi^2 (12n^2 \sqrt{5})^{-1} \{1 + o(n^{-2})\}. \qquad (3.46)$$

3.33 This method would also apply when the distance between the parallel lines is not small enough to justify the above approximation, but the calculations then get considerably more complicated and we shall describe here only the classical case of a single needle. Suppose as before that the distance between the parallel lines is unity and that the needle has length $L > 1$. Write $P_0, P_1, P_2, \ldots$ for the probabilities of $0, 1, 2, \ldots$ intersections. We have already found P_0 in (3.44). Suppose that $L = n + l$, where $l < 1$. Then there can be $0, 1, \ldots, n+1$ intersections. Define $\alpha_1, \alpha_2, \ldots, \alpha_n$ to be angles such that

$$L\sin\alpha_1 = 1, \quad L\sin\alpha_2 = 2, \ldots, \quad L\sin\alpha_n = n.$$

Consider now P_{n+1}. In order to obtain $n+1$ intersections, θ must lie between α_n and $\frac{1}{2}\pi$ (Fig. 3.7).

For fixed θ we then see by considering two possible positions of the end of the needle that the probability of $n+1$ intersections is $L\sin\theta - n$. P_{n+1} is therefore equal to

$$\frac{2}{\pi} \int_{\alpha_n}^{\frac{1}{2}\pi} (L\sin\theta - n) = 2L\pi^{-1}\cos\alpha_n + 2n\pi^{-1}(\alpha_n - \tfrac{1}{2}\pi). \qquad (3.47)$$

For k intersections to occur $(0 < k < n+1)$ it is necessary that θ should lie in the range $(\alpha_{k-1}, \alpha_{k+1})$ and we must consider the cases $(\alpha_{k-1} < \theta \leqslant \alpha_k)$ and $(\alpha_k < \theta \leqslant \alpha_{k+1})$ separately. In the first, the conditional probability of k intersections is $L\sin\theta - (k-1)$, and in the second

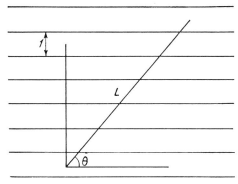

Fig. 3.7

it is $(k+1) - L$. Thus the total probability is

$$P_k = \frac{2}{\pi} \int_{\alpha_{k-1}}^{\alpha_k} \{L \sin\theta - (k-1)\} \, d\theta + \frac{2}{\pi} \int_{\alpha_k}^{\alpha_{k+1}} \{k+1 - L \sin\theta\} \, d\theta,$$

$$= \frac{2}{\pi} \{(k+1)\,\alpha_{k+1} - 2k\,\alpha_k + (k-1)\,\alpha_{k-1}\},$$

$$+ \frac{2L}{\pi} \{\cos\alpha_{k+1} - 2\cos\alpha_k + \cos\alpha_{k-1}\}, \tag{3.48}$$

except when $k = n$ for which we have to put $\alpha_{k+1} = \frac{1}{2}\pi$.

3.34 It is also possible to consider the probability of a needle, thrown at random, intersecting one of two sets of parallel lines which are at right angles to each other. If they are distant a and b apart and $L < a, L < b$ then the probability that the needle crosses at least one line is

$$\frac{2L}{\pi} \{a^{-1} + b^{-1} - 2L\,(ab)^{-1}\}. \tag{3.49}$$

This and various similar results are easily obtained (see amongst others Deltheil, 1926, Mantel 1953).

Random lines in three dimensions

3.35 The theory of random straight lines in three-dimensional space leads to a variety of problems some of which are analogous to those considered above. We have already seen in Chapter 1 that if lines are represented by four coordinates (a, b, p, q), so that a line is determined by the equations

$$x = az + p,$$
$$y = bz + q,$$

then the appropriate measure to use is defined by the element

$$(1 + a^2 + b^2)^{-2}\, da\, db\, dp\, dq. \tag{3.50}$$

This differential element implies that if we suppose that lines are defined by their intersection P with some plane, then P must be uniformly distributed at random over the plane and, independently of this, all directions are equally likely. Consider then the measure of the set of all lines which intersect a certain measurable set E lying in some plane which we can take as the plane $Z = 0$. Then the measure of such lines will equal the measure of E multiplied by the integral

$$\int_0^\infty \int_0^\infty \frac{da\, db}{(1 + a^2 + b^2)^2} = \pi. \tag{3.51}$$

Hence the measure of all lines intersecting a plane region of area A is πA. Since almost any line meets a three-dimensional convex region in two points, the measure of all lines meeting such a figure is $\frac{1}{2}\pi S$, where S is the surface area of the figure. This can be interpreted in another way. Let $P(\mathbf{n})$ be the area of the projection of the convex region on any plane with normal $\mathbf{n}$, so that $\bar{P}$, the mean of this projection for all $\mathbf{n}$, is

$$\bar{P} = (4\pi)^{-1} \int\int P(\mathbf{n})\, d\omega, \tag{3.52}$$

where $d\omega$ is the element of solid angle corresponding to $\mathbf{n}$. Then $2\pi\bar{P}$ is the measure of all lines meeting the convex region (because each line is counted only once, whatever its "direction", and the possible directions fill a solid angle of size 2π), and equating this to the previous value we have $S = 4\bar{P}$, which is "Cauchy's formula" for the area of a convex body. This provides a useful practical method for measuring the surface areas of small convex bodies such as stones. This method is the three-dimensional analogue of Steinhaus' method described earlier in this chapter, and a similar set of inequalities can be established for finite approximations (Moran, 1944). In fact, if $\bar{P}$ is the true mean value given by (3.52) and P_1, P_2 are the means of the projections of the convex body on the faces of a dodecahedron and icosahedron respectively, then

$$0.91758 \leqslant P_1 \bar{P}^{-1} \leqslant 1.07869$$
$$0.9560 \;\; \leqslant P_2 \bar{P}^{-1} \leqslant 1.0472, \tag{3.53}$$

these limits being five- and four-figure values of expressions which are best possible limits.

3.36 The "isepiphanic" theorem states that of all closed surfaces in three-dimensional space which are topologically equivalent to a sphere, and for which a surface area can be defined, the ratio $S^3 V^{-2}$ (V = volume) is a minimum for a sphere. This is a very difficult theorem to prove in general, but it is relatively easy when confined to the class of convex surfaces. In that case it may be put in the form that $\bar{P}^3 V^{-2}$ is a minimum for a sphere. Now, for any closed surface, $S \geqslant 4\bar{P}$—where $\bar{P}$ is the mean projection on a random plane (each point in the projection being counted once only, even if more than two points of the surface project on to it)—and it may therefore be conjectured that for any set E in space whose projection $P(\mathbf{n}, E)$ in the direction $\mathbf{n}$ has a surface measure which is a measurable function of $\mathbf{n}$, $\bar{P}^3 V^{-2}$ is a minimum for the sphere, where $\bar{P}$ is the mean value of $P(\mathbf{n}, E)$ in all directions and V is the three-dimensional Lebesgue measure of E. This has not been proved.

3.37 The second moment—or better the variance—of $P(\mathbf{n})$ for a convex body is also a number which characterizes the convex body. It is clearly zero for a sphere and has been calculated for a circular cylinder and a rectangular parallelepiped by Walters (1947).

3.38 A further consequence of the above results is that if K_1 is a convex region contained in a convex region K_2, the probability that a random secant of K_2 intersects K_1 is $S_1 S_2{}^{-1}$, where S_1, S_2 are the surface areas of K_1 and K_2. In particular the probability that a random chord of a sphere intersects a given diametral plane inside the sphere is $2\pi (4\pi)^{-1} = \frac{1}{2}$, since the circular area formed by the diametral plane can be regarded as a flat convex region with surface area 2π, the radius being taken as unity.

3.39 With the probability element (3.50) we have, in effect, defined the line by its intersection with a fixed plane, and its direction. The above discussion suggests that it would also be valuable to define a line first by its direction and then by its intersection with some plane perpendicular to its direction, this representation being analogous to the use of the polar coordinates of a line in the plane. Thus, consider the plane

$$ax + by + Z = 0$$

which is perpendicular to the line given by

$$x = az + p,$$
$$y = bz + q.$$

The direction cosines of the line are

$$l = a(1 + a^2 + b^2)^{-\frac{1}{2}}, \quad m = b(1 + a^2 + b^2)^{-\frac{1}{2}}, \quad \text{and} \quad n = (1 + a^2 + b^2)^{-\frac{1}{2}}.$$

The direction being fixed, an element of area in this plane will be got by varying p and q and is given by

$$dS = (1 + a^2 + b^2)^{\frac{1}{2}} \, dp \, dq = n^{-1} dp \, dq. \tag{3.54}$$

To obtain the element of solid angle, write

$$l = \sin\theta \cos\phi,$$
$$m = \sin\theta \sin\phi,$$
$$n = \cos\theta,$$

so that the element of solid angle is

$$d\Omega = \sin\theta \, d\theta \, d\phi = \frac{\cos\theta \sin\theta \, d\theta \, d\phi}{n_1}. \tag{3.55}$$

The Jacobian of l and m with respect to θ and ϕ is

$$\frac{\partial(l, m)}{\partial(\theta, \phi)} = \begin{vmatrix} \cos\theta \cos\phi & -\sin\theta \sin\phi \\ \cos\theta \sin\phi & \sin\theta \cos\phi \end{vmatrix}$$
$$= \cos\theta \sin\theta, \tag{3.56}$$

so that the element of solid angle is $n^{-1} dl \, dm$, and taking the Jacobian of l, m with respect to a and b we get

$$n^{-3} da \, db = \frac{da \, db}{(1 + a^2 + b^2)^{\frac{3}{2}}}. \tag{3.57}$$

Thus $dS \, d\Omega$, where $d\Omega$ is the element of solid angle, is equal to (3.50).

Mean length of secants of a convex body

3.40 Now consider the mean length of secants of a convex body. Let K be the body and $K(\mathbf{n})$ its two-dimensional projection in the direction $\mathbf{n}$. The integral of the length of a secant in the direction $\mathbf{n}$ taken over all its points of intersection in $K(\mathbf{n})$ is clearly the volume of K, and the mean length is $VP(\mathbf{n})^{-1}$, where $P(\mathbf{n})$ is the area of $K(\mathbf{n})$. Weighting this by $P(\mathbf{n})$ and integrating over all directions, we get V. But the measure of all secants is the integral of $P(\mathbf{n})$ over all directions, which is $\frac{1}{4}S$. Thus the mean length of a secant is $4VS^{-1}$.

3.41 This result has some application in architectural acoustics as a measure of the mean free path in a room (Bate and Pillow, 1947). Suppose the wavelength to be so small that the sound-waves can be considered to travel in straight lines until reaching the walls, when they are reflected in the usual manner. Let P be the point inside the room which is emitting sound-waves uniformly in all directions. Taking one of these directions, we may suppose the path of the sound-wave to extend for a long distance which, when divided by the number of reflections, will give the mean free path in that direction from the point P. Averaging over all directions we obtain the mean free path from the point P. In general this will depend on the point P. Bate and Pillow show that for a room in the form of a rectangular parallelepiped the mean free path is independent of P and equal to $4VS^{-1}$, the mean length of a secant. For a sphere of radius a with the point P at a distance b from the centre the mean free path is

$$4b\left\{\ln\frac{a+b}{a-b}\right\}^{-1}. \tag{3.58}$$

Averaged over a uniform distribution in the sphere this is again $4VS^{-1}$. For a cylinder the mean free path also depends on P, but averaged over all points the result is $4VS^{-1}$. Thus it appears to be a general rule that the mean free path obtained by repeated reflection is equal to the length of a random secant of the body, but this has not been proved in general.

3.42 Buffon's problem can also be generalized by considering a "needle" of length L placed at random in space in which there are an infinite number of parallel planes unit distance apart. Suppose first that $L < 1$. Using polar coordinates for the direction of the needle, the axis of coordinates being perpendicular to the planes, the probability element is

$$(4\pi)^{-1}\sin\theta\,d\theta\,d\phi \tag{3.59}$$

in the usual notation. Integrating over ϕ, this can be written $\frac{1}{2}d(\cos\theta)$. Hence the projection of the needle on a line perpendicular to the planes is an interval of length l, where l has a uniform distribution on the interval $(0, L)$. Since the position of this interval is random, the probability of an intersection for any given orientation is l which, averaged over the distribution of orientations, gives $\frac{1}{2}L$ for the required probability. Similarly the distribution of the number of intersections for $L > 1$ is easy to find, and in any case it is obvious that the expected number of intersections is $\frac{1}{2}L$.

3.43 As for the case of random lines in a plane intersecting convex figures, it is possible to construct a theory of the intersection of random lines in three dimensions with convex regions which enables inferences about these regions to be drawn from knowledge of the intersections. This is more conveniently studied in the next chapter, in connection with the theory of intersections of random planes with convex figures.

CHAPTER 4

RANDOM PLANES AND RANDOM ROTATIONS

Random planes

4.1 We have already seen in Chapter 1 that the appropriate element of measure for planes defined by the polar equation

$$x \sin\theta \cos\phi + y \sin\theta \sin\phi + z \cos\theta = p$$

is

$$\sin\theta \, d\theta \, d\phi \, dp, \tag{4.1}$$

and that if we use the representation

$$ux + vy + wz + 1 = 0,$$

the corresponding element of measure is

$$\frac{du \, dv \, dw}{(u^2 + v^2 + w^2)^2}. \tag{4.2}$$

From these results we can obtain the measures of the sets of planes which satisfy any specified conditions. Thus consider the set of all planes which intersect a linear segment of length L. Take this segment along the z-axis and use polar coordinates. Then p will be uniformly distributed between 0 and $L \cos\theta$. The measure of the set of planes will thus be

$$\int_0^{2\pi} d\phi \int_0^{\frac{\pi}{2}} \sin\theta \int_0^{L\cos\theta} dp \, d\theta = \pi L. \tag{4.3}$$

This can be generalized to a twisted curve of length L. Let $N(\theta, \phi, p)$ be the number of intersections of a plane of coordinates (θ, ϕ, p) with the curve. Then by breaking up the curve into a set of nearly linear elements and adding we see that

$$\iiint N(\theta, \phi, p) \, d\theta \, d\phi \, dp = \pi L. \tag{4.4}$$

4.2 (4.4) can be given another interpretation. Consider the projection of the curve on a plane perpendicular to the vector direction **n** and suppose this has length $L(\mathbf{n})$. Let $\bar{L}$ be the average of $L(\mathbf{n})$ over all directions so that

$$\bar{L} = \frac{1}{4\pi} \iint L(\mathbf{n}) \, dw,$$

where dw is the element of solid angle. Then by splitting up the curve into small parts which are approximately linear we see that

$$\bar{L} = 2\pi^{-1}L. \tag{4.5}$$

This result can be obtained from the previous one. For consider the curve projected on the plane perpendicular to **n**. This has length $L(\mathbf{n})$ which by (3.4) is equal to $\frac{1}{2}\pi$ multiplied by the average number of intersections of the twisted curve with random planes perpendicular to the plane of projection. If we now integrate over all directions of **n** we see that

$$\bar{L} = (4\pi)^{-1}\int L(\mathbf{n})\,dw = (2\pi)^{-1}L,$$

because in integrating over all directions of **n** we have counted each plane in space twice, thus providing a factor 2π.

4.3 This result is similar to Steinhaus' result (Chapter 3) and it is curious that (as pointed out by Santaló, 1946) it is possible to prove results similar to (3.53) for the average length of the projections on the face of a dodecahedron or icosahedron. Let $\bar{L}_1$ and $\bar{L}_2$ be the mean projections in these two cases. Then, as in (3.53),

$$0\cdot91758 \leqslant \bar{L}_1(\bar{L})^{-1} \leqslant 1\cdot07869,$$
$$0\cdot9560 \;\leqslant \bar{L}_2(\bar{L})^{-1} \leqslant 1\cdot0472. \tag{4.6}$$

To see this it is first clearly sufficient to prove these inequalities when the curve is a straight line. This we can replace by a thin cylinder of diameter d, where d is small. Except for a small error term, the areal projections and surface area of this cylinder are proportional to the length, and by using the previous theorem the result follows. However, in this case the inequalities (4.6) are not the best possible and the best inequalities have not been established.

Planes intersecting a curve

4.4 Now consider the measure of the set of all planes which intersect a closed convex curve C lying in a fixed plane. Since every plane which intersects this curve must do so in two points, we see from (4.4) that the measure of all such planes is $\frac{1}{2}\pi L$, where L is the perimeter of C.

4.5 Before extending this to the measure of planes intersecting convex figures in general, we describe another result, due to Barbier (1860), which generalizes more simply. Instead of obtaining the measure of all planes which intersect the plane convex figures, we obtain the integral, over the set of all such planes, of the length of the intersection. Suppose that such a plane is given by

$$x \sin \theta \cos \phi + y \sin \theta \sin \phi + z \cos \theta = p$$

and that the fixed plane is $z = 0$. The line of intersection is given by

$$z = 0, \quad x \cos \phi + y \sin \phi = \frac{p}{\sin \theta}.$$

Let C be the length of the chord formed by this line, so that

$$\int \frac{C \, dp}{\sin \theta} = S, \text{ the area of the convex figure.}$$

Then the total integral over all intersecting planes is

$$\iiint C \sin \theta \, dp \, d\theta \, d\phi = \int_0^{2\pi} d\phi \int_0^{\frac{\pi}{2}} \sin^2 \theta \, d\theta \int \frac{C \, dp}{\sin \theta}$$

$$= 2\pi S \int_0^{\frac{\pi}{2}} \sin^2 \theta \, d\theta = \tfrac{1}{2}\pi^2 S. \tag{4.7}$$

This approach ascribes to each plane a weight equal to the length of its intersection with the plane convex figure. If we have any reasonably regular surface in space with finite area, and $L(\theta, \phi, p)$ is the length of the curve of intersection with any plane, the integral of L over the set of all intersecting planes is equal to the surface area multiplied by $\tfrac{1}{2}\pi^2$.

Planes intersecting a convex region

4.6 Now consider the measure of all planes meeting a convex region K in space. Keeping θ and ϕ fixed, the integral is equal to the length of the projection of the figure on a line in the direction (θ, ϕ). This length may be called the "thickness" (*épaisseur*, *Breite*) of the figure in the direction (θ, ϕ). The measure of all planes meeting K is therefore

$$J = \tfrac{1}{2} \iint T(\theta, \phi) \sin \theta \, d\theta \, d\phi, \tag{4.8}$$

where $T(\theta, \phi)$ is the thickness in the direction (θ, ϕ) and the integral is taken over all directions. If K is replaced by a convex figure in a plane we have seen that J is equal to $\tfrac{1}{2}\pi L$, where L is the perimeter of the convex figure. By analogy with this case E. Cartan (1896) proposed that $2\pi^{-1} J$ be called the "perimeter" of the convex figure K. Minkowski (1903) has shown (and we prove below) that

$$J = M = \tfrac{1}{2} \iint (\rho_1^{-1} + \rho_2^{-1}) \, dS, \tag{4.9}$$

where K is sufficiently regular for the two principal radii of curvature to exist and be integrable, dS is the element of surface area, and the integral is taken over the whole surface. Having found M it then follows from the above that the mean length of the perimeter of the intersection of K by an arbitrary plane is

$$\tfrac{1}{2}\pi^2 SM^{-1},$$

and since the volume, V, of K is obtained by integrating the area of the intersection over all possible planes and multiplying by $(2\pi)^{-1}$, the mean area of intersection is

$$2\pi V M^{-1}. \tag{4.10}$$

Minkowski's theorem

4.7 We now prove (4.9) directly by the method given by Deltheil. Taking the origin of polar coordinates inside K and writing

$$\alpha = \sin\theta\cos\phi, \quad \beta = \sin\theta\sin\phi, \quad \gamma = \cos\theta$$

for the direction cosines of a vector issuing from the origin, we see that the tangent plane, or plane of support, is given by

$$\alpha x + \beta y + \gamma z = H(\theta, \phi), \tag{4.11}$$

where $H(\theta, \phi)$ is the function of support, so that J is the integral of H over all directions. Suppose that the tangent plane always touches the surface at a single point M (when this is not true the result can be obtained by a limiting process). The coordinates of M can be obtained in terms of θ and ϕ by solving (4.11), and the two equations obtained by differentiating (4.11) with respect to θ and ϕ. We get in this way

$$x = H\sin\theta\cos\phi + \frac{\partial H}{\partial\theta}\cos\theta\cos\phi - \frac{\partial H}{\partial\phi}\frac{\sin\phi}{\sin\theta},$$

$$y = H\sin\theta\sin\phi + \frac{\partial H}{\partial\theta}\cos\theta\sin\phi + \frac{\partial H}{\partial\phi}\frac{\cos\phi}{\cos\theta},$$

$$z = H\cos\theta - \frac{\partial H}{\partial\theta}\sin\theta. \tag{4.12}$$

The form of these equations shows that the line from the origin perpendicular to the plane of support can be regarded as having components

$$H, \quad \frac{\partial H}{\partial\theta}, \quad (\sin\theta)^{-1}\frac{\partial H}{\partial\phi}$$

relative to orthogonal coordinate axes whose direction cosines are given by

$$(\alpha, \beta, \gamma) = (\sin\theta\cos\phi, \sin\theta\sin\phi, \cos\theta),$$

$$(\alpha', \beta', \gamma') = (\cos\theta\cos\phi, \cos\theta\sin\phi, -\sin\theta),$$

$$(\alpha'', \beta'', \gamma'') = (-\sin\phi, \cos\phi, 0). \tag{4.13}$$

At the tangent point M there will be two lines of curvature each with its own principal radius of curvature. Let ρ be one of these. By a

G.P.—F

standard formula in differential geometry it follows that for a displacement along the corresponding line of curvature we have

$$\frac{dx}{d\alpha} = \frac{dy}{d\beta} = \frac{dz}{d\gamma} = -\rho.$$

Hence along this line of curvature ϕ will be a function of θ such that

$$\frac{d\phi}{d\theta} = \frac{\dfrac{\partial x}{\partial \theta} - \rho\dfrac{\partial \alpha}{\partial \theta}}{\dfrac{\partial x}{\partial \phi} - \rho\dfrac{\partial \alpha}{\partial \phi}} = \frac{\dfrac{\partial y}{\partial \theta} - \rho\dfrac{\partial \beta}{\partial \theta}}{\dfrac{\partial y}{\partial \phi} - \rho\dfrac{\partial \beta}{\partial \phi}} = \frac{\dfrac{\partial z}{\partial \theta} - \rho\dfrac{\partial \gamma}{\partial \theta}}{\dfrac{\partial z}{\partial \phi} - \rho\dfrac{\partial \gamma}{\partial \phi}} \tag{4.14}$$

The vector (α, β, γ) is in the direction of the perpendicular on the plane of support and is therefore at right angles to the infinitesimal displacements of P when θ and ϕ vary. Hence

$$\alpha\frac{\partial x}{\partial \theta} + \beta\frac{\partial y}{\partial \theta} + \gamma\frac{\partial z}{\partial \theta} = 0,$$

$$\alpha\frac{\partial x}{\partial \phi} + \beta\frac{\partial y}{\partial \phi} + \gamma\frac{\partial z}{\partial \phi} = 0. \tag{4.15}$$

Differentiating these with respect to θ and ϕ using (4.13) we get

$$0 = \Sigma\alpha\frac{\partial^2 x}{\partial \theta^2} + \Sigma\alpha'\frac{\partial x}{\partial \theta} = \Sigma\alpha\frac{\partial^2 x}{\partial \theta^2} + R, \text{ say.}$$

$$0 = \Sigma\alpha\frac{\partial^2 x}{\partial \theta \partial \phi} + \sin\theta\,\Sigma\alpha''\frac{\partial x}{\partial \theta},$$

$$= \Sigma\alpha\frac{\partial^2 x}{\partial \theta \partial \phi} + S\sin\theta, \text{ say,}$$

$$= \Sigma\alpha\frac{\partial^2 x}{\partial \theta \partial \phi} + \Sigma\alpha'\frac{\partial x}{\partial \phi}.$$

$$0 = \Sigma\alpha\frac{\partial^2 x}{\partial \phi^2} + \sin\theta\,\Sigma\alpha''\frac{\partial x}{\partial \phi},$$

$$= \Sigma\alpha\frac{\partial^2 x}{\partial \phi^2} + T\sin^2\theta, \text{ say.} \tag{4.16}$$

Multiplying the last three ratios in (4.14) by α, β, γ (or α', β', γ') in the numerator and denominator and adding, we therefore get

$$\frac{R - \rho}{S\sin\theta} = \frac{S}{(T - \rho)\sin\theta}$$

from which we obtain the quadratic equation

$$\rho^2 - (R + T)\rho + RT - S^2 = 0. \tag{4.17}$$

To find R, T, and S in terms of θ and ϕ we differentiate (4.11) with respect to θ keeping x, y, and z fixed, and then again with respect to θ allowing x, y, and z to vary, obtaining

$$R = \Sigma \alpha' \frac{\partial x}{\partial \theta} = H + \frac{\partial^2 H}{\partial \theta^2}. \tag{4.18}$$

Differentiating with respect to ϕ and allowing x, y, and z to vary, we get

$$S = (\sin \theta)^{-1} \frac{\partial^2 H}{\partial \theta\, \partial \phi} - \cos \theta (\sin \theta)^{-2} \frac{\partial H}{\partial \phi}. \tag{4.19}$$

Differentiating (4.10) with respect to ϕ we get

$$\Sigma \alpha'' x = (\sin \theta)^{-1} \frac{\partial H}{\partial \phi} \tag{4.20}$$

and differentiating again, letting x, y, and z vary, we get

$$T \sin \theta - x \cos \phi - y \sin \phi = (\sin \theta)^{-1} \frac{\partial^2 H}{\partial \phi^2}, \tag{4.21}$$

and therefore

$$T = H + \frac{\partial H}{\partial \theta} \cot \theta + (\sin \theta)^{-1} \frac{\partial^2 H}{\partial \phi^2}.$$

From this

$$\tfrac{1}{2} (\rho_1^{-1} + \rho_2^{-1})$$
$$= (RT - S^2)^{-1} \left\{ H + \tfrac{1}{2} \frac{\partial H}{\partial \theta} \cot \theta + \tfrac{1}{2} \frac{\partial^2 H}{\partial \theta^2} + \tfrac{1}{2} (\sin \theta)^{-2} \frac{\partial^2 H}{\partial \phi^2} \right\}. \tag{4.22}$$

The lines of curvature are orthogonal, and if we represent an element of area on the surface around the point M by $d\sigma$ we have

$$d\sigma = (\rho_1 \rho_2)^{-1} d\Omega,$$

where $d\Omega$ is the corresponding element of solid angle traced out by the vector in the direction (θ, ϕ). Minkowski's theorem then takes the form

$$\iint H \sin \theta\, d\theta\, d\phi$$

$$= \tfrac{1}{2} \iint (\rho_1^{-1} + \rho_2^{-1})\, d\sigma$$

$$= \tfrac{1}{2} \iint (\rho_1 + \rho_2) \sin \theta\, d\theta\, d\phi$$

$$= \iint \tfrac{1}{2} (R + T) \sin \theta\, d\theta\, d\phi$$

$$= \iint \left\{ H + \tfrac{1}{2} \frac{\partial H}{\partial \theta} \cot \theta + \tfrac{1}{2} \frac{\partial^2 H}{\partial \theta^2} + \tfrac{1}{2} (\sin \theta)^{-2} \frac{\partial^2 H}{\partial \phi^2} \right\} \sin \theta\, d\theta\, d\phi, \tag{4.23}$$

where $0 \leqslant \theta \leqslant \pi$, $0 \leqslant \phi \leqslant 2\pi$. To prove the result it is therefore sufficient to show that

$$A = \int\int (\sin\theta)^{-1} \frac{\partial^2 H}{\partial\phi^2} \, d\theta \, d\phi = 0, \tag{4.24}$$

and

$$B = \int\int \left\{ \cos\theta \frac{\partial H}{\partial\theta} + \sin\theta \frac{\partial^2 H}{\partial\theta^2} \right\} d\theta \, d\phi = 0. \tag{4.25}$$

A is zero, since after integrating with respect to ϕ we get $\dfrac{\partial H}{\partial\phi}$ which is periodic. In B we integrate first with respect to θ and obtain

$$\sin\theta \frac{\partial H}{\partial\theta}, \tag{4.26}$$

which is zero at $\theta = 0, \pi$. Thus Minkowski's formula is demonstrated.

4.8 It follows that if K_1 is a convex body interior to K, and M_{K_1} and M_K the corresponding integrals (4.10), the probability that a random plane intersecting K also intersects K_1 is

$$M_{K_1} M_K^{-1}. \tag{4.27}$$

This is the spatial analogue of the similar result for plane figures implied by formula (3.2).

Some further results

4.9 We can obtain a number of other means and probabilities in this way (Hostinsky, 1925). For example, we have seen from (4.7) that if L is the length of the perimeter of the intersection of a plane with K, the integral of L over all intersecting planes is $\frac{1}{2}\pi^2 S$. Hence the mean perimeter is $\frac{1}{2}\pi^2 S M^{-1}$. Similarly, since the integral of the area of intersection over all intersecting planes is $2\pi V$, where V is the volume of K, the mean area of intersection is $2\pi V M^{-1}$.

4.10 Now consider two independently random planes both intersecting K. The measure of all such planes (counting them as distinguishable) is M^2. To obtain the probability that their line of intersection intersects K we have to find the measure of all such pairs satisfying this property. Suppose one of them is fixed and has an intersection with K whose perimeter is L. Then the measure of planes which intersect this intersection is $\frac{1}{2}\pi L$ from (4.3). On the other hand we have seen that the integral of L over all intersecting planes is $\frac{1}{2}\pi^2 S$, so that the measure of all pairs of planes intersecting K and whose intersection intersects K is $\frac{1}{4}\pi^3 S$. Thus the probability of two planes which intersect K having an intersection which intersects K is

$$\frac{\pi^3 S}{4M}. \tag{4.28}$$

4.11 Now consider the probability that three planes intersecting K have their common point inside K. The measure of all triples of intersecting planes is M^3 (regarding the planes as distinguishable, so that each geometric triple is counted six times). Suppose two of these planes intersect inside K. The measure of all planes which intersect this intersection is πC, where C is the length of the intersection. The integral of C over all positions of one of these planes is $\frac{1}{2}\pi^2 S$, where S is the area of intersection of the other plane. In turn, the integral of S is $2\pi V$. Hence the measure of all such triples is $\pi^4 V$, and the required probability is

$$\frac{\pi^4 V}{M^3}. \tag{4.29}$$

4.12 We have already seen that the mean value of the length of the intersection made by a random line intersecting K is $4VS^{-1}$. Let such a chord have length C. Then it is possible to find some of the higher moments of C. Hostinsky (1925) has obtained the fourth moment. Consider two points A_1 and A_2 inside K and with coordinates (x_1, y_1, z_1) and (x_2, y_2, z_2). Then

$$V^2 = \int\int\int\int\int\int dx_1\, dy_1\, dz_1\, dx_2\, dy_2\, dz_2. \tag{4.30}$$

Let A_1 be fixed for the moment and let a line through it form a chord of length C, A_1 being at a distance r from one end of the chord and $C - r$ from the other. Suppose A_1 is the vertex of a cone surrounding the chord and having a small solid angle $d\Omega$. Integrating with respect to (x_2, y_2, z_2) over the volume of this cone, we obtain

$$\tfrac{1}{3}\{r^3 + (C-r)^3\}\, d\Omega. \tag{4.31}$$

We can choose the coordinates of A_1 in such a way that one corresponds to the direction of the chord and the other two are perpendicular and form an element of area dQ. Then

$$V^2 = \tfrac{1}{3}\int\int\int\int\left\{\int_0^r (r^3 + (C-r)^3)\, dr\right\} dQ\, d\Omega$$

$$= \tfrac{1}{6}\int\int\int C^4\, dQ\, d\Omega. \tag{4.32}$$

From the previous results we see that

$$\int\int\int\int dQ\, d\Omega = \tfrac{1}{2}\pi S,\qquad(4.33)$$

and hence the mean value of C^4 is

$$12V^2(\pi S)^{-1}.\qquad(4.34)$$

4.13 Hostinsky considers some other means of a similar kind and also the analogue in three dimensions of Sylvester's quadrilateral problem, i.e. given five points chosen at random inside a convex body K, to obtain the probability that none lies inside the tetrahedron formed by the other four.

Distribution of sizes of particles

4.14 We now consider the problem of determining the distribution of the sizes of particles embedded in an opaque medium from the measurement of the figures formed by their intersections with a random plane, or from the segments formed by their intersection with a random line. This problem has application in a number of scientific fields, and has been considered by a number of authors, some of them independently, e.g. Wicksell (1925, 1926), Scheil (1931), Fullman (1953), Reid (1955), Santaló (1955), and Krumbein and Pettijohn (1938).

4.15 Suppose first that the particles are all spherical and distributed in such a way that the mean number of centres in unit volume is λ. We can treat the centres as being distributed in a Poisson field, although the spheres are non-overlapping since the plane of intersection is itself chosen at random. Let the probability distribution of the diameters have density $F(r)$, so that (r being used for a *diameter*)

$$\int_0^a F(r)\, dr$$

is the probability of a sphere chosen at random having a diameter less than a. The expected number of spheres whose diameters lie in the range $(r, r+dr)$ and which intersect an arbitrary plane in a unit area of the latter will be $\lambda r F(r)\, dr$, and hence the probability density of the distribution of diameters of spheres which intersect the plane will be

$$f(r) = \frac{rF(r)}{\displaystyle\int_0^\infty rF(r)\, dr} = \frac{rF(r)}{r_0},\qquad(4.35)$$

where r_0 is the mean diameter of a sphere chosen at random.

If a sphere of diameter r does intersect the plane, the probability that its centre lies at a distance y from the plane is $2r^{-1}\, dy$ $(0 \leqslant y \leqslant \tfrac{1}{2}r)$, and the diameter x of the circle of intersection is $(r^2 - 4y^2)$. Hence the expected number of spheres having diameters in the range $(r, r + dr)$ and intersecting the plane in a circle of diameter x whose centre lies in a unit area is

$$\lambda r_0^{-1} F(r) \times (r^2 - x^2)^{-\frac{1}{2}} \, dr \, dx. \tag{4.36}$$

The probability distribution, $\phi(r) \, dr$, of the diameters of the circle of intersection when it is known that the sphere does intersect the plane is therefore

$$\phi(x) \, dx = \frac{x}{r_0} \int_x^\infty \frac{F(r)}{\sqrt{(r^2 - x^2)}} \, dr \, dx. \tag{4.37}$$

Since $\phi(x)$ can be found by observation, we have to determine $F(r)$ by the integral equation

$$\phi(x) = \frac{x}{r_0} \int_x^\infty \frac{F(r)}{\sqrt{(r^2 - x^2)}} \, dr. \tag{4.38}$$

Write $F(r) = r F_1(r^2)$ and we obtain

$$\phi(x) = \frac{x}{2r_0} \int_{x^2}^\infty \frac{F_1(z) \, dz}{\sqrt{(z - x^2)}}, \tag{4.39}$$

which is an integral equation of Abel's type (Courant and Hilbert, 1931, p. 134) whose solution is

$$F_1(z) = -2\pi^{-1} \int_x^\infty (x^2 - z)^{-\frac{1}{2}} r_0 \frac{d}{dx} (x^{-1} \phi(x)) \, x \, dx, \tag{4.40}$$

from which we obtain

$$F(r) = -\frac{2r r_0}{\pi} \int_{x^2}^\infty (x^2 - r^2)^{-\frac{1}{2}} \frac{d}{dx} (x^{-1} \phi(x)) \, dx. \tag{4.41}$$

Given observations of the diameters of the circles we can estimate the distribution $\phi(x)$ and hence calculate $F(x)$ from (4.41). For numerical work it is probably best to integrate (4.41) by parts first, so as to avoid having to estimate a derivative.

4.16 $F(r)$ and $\phi(x)$ are both the densities of probability distributions, and it is interesting to express the moments of one distribution in terms of those of the other. Let M_n and m_n be these moments, so that

$$M_n = \int_0^\infty r^n F(r) \, dr, \quad m_n = \int_0^\infty x^n \phi(x) \, dx. \tag{4.42}$$

Using (4.37) we have

$$m_n = \int_0^\infty x^n \phi(x) \, dx = r_0^{-1} \int_0^\infty x^{n+1} \int_x^\infty (r^2 - x^2)^{-\frac{1}{2}} F(r) \, dr \, dx, \tag{4.43}$$

and inverting the order of integration (which can be justified) we get

$$m_n = r_0^{-1} \int_0^\infty r^{n+1} F(r)\, dr \int_0^1 w^{n+1}(1-w^2)^{-\frac{1}{2}}\, dw. \qquad (4.44)$$

The second integral is of the form

$$\int_0^{\frac{1}{2}\pi} \sin^n \theta\, d\theta = \frac{2.4.6.\ldots n-1}{3.5.\ldots n}, \quad \text{if } n \text{ is odd},$$

$$= \frac{1.3.\ldots n-1}{2.4.\ldots n}\cdot\frac{\pi}{2}, \quad \text{if } n \text{ is even},$$

$$= J_n, \text{ say}.$$

Then

$$m_n = r_0^{-1} J_{n+1} M_{n+1} = J_{n+1} M^{-1} M_{n+1}, \qquad (4.45)$$

since $r_0 = M_1$. This provides us with another method of determining the distribution, since if we can estimate $m_1, m_2, \ldots$ from the observations, we can find $M_2 M_1^{-1}, M_3 M_1^{-1}, \ldots$ and there remains only the problem of finding $M_1 = r_0$. One way of doing this is to use the fact that r_0, the mean of the diameters of the spheres, is equal to $\frac{1}{2}\pi$ times the harmonic mean of the observed diameters. To prove this we have $r_0\{\text{harmonic mean of observed diameters}\}$

$$= r_0 \int_0^\infty \phi(x) x^{-1}\, dx = \int_0^\infty \int_x^\infty (r^2 - x^2)^{-\frac{1}{2}} F(r)\, dr\, dx$$

$$= \int_0^\infty dr \int_0^r F(r)(r^2 - x^2)^{-\frac{1}{2}}\, dx = \frac{1}{2}\pi \int_0^\infty F(r)\, dr = \frac{1}{2}\pi.$$

It is also interesting to note that it is possible for the distributions of true diameter and observed diameter to coincide, i.e. for $\phi(x) = F(x)$. This occurs when

$$F(x) = \frac{x}{\sigma^2}\exp-\frac{x^2}{2\sigma^2}, \qquad (4.46)$$

for then

$$r_0 = \sigma\left(\tfrac{1}{2}\pi\right)^{\frac{1}{2}},$$

and by (4.19)

$$\phi(x) = \frac{x}{\sigma\left(\tfrac{1}{2}\pi\right)^{\frac{1}{2}}} \int_x^\infty \frac{x}{\sigma^2}(r^2 - x^2)^{-\frac{1}{2}}\exp-\frac{r^2}{2\sigma^2}\, dr$$

$$= \frac{x}{\sigma^2}\exp-\frac{x^2}{2\sigma^2}.$$

Equation (4.38) also occurs in the theory of the "globular cluster problem" in astronomy (Wicksell, 1925). A globular cluster is a collection of stars arranged around a common centre in spherical layers of equal density. The relationship between the density in these layers as a function of the radial distance and the density in a circular ring in the projection on a plane is again given by an integral equation of the form (4.38).

4.17 We also see that it is possible to set up an analogous theory for circles in a plane cut by random straight lines, and this links up with the investigations of McIntyre described in Chapter 3. The resulting integral equation (which is obtained by Reid, 1955) is again of Abel's type and can be solved by similar methods.

4.18 Wicksell (1926) has considered the case of ellipsoidal particles. Suppose these are all of the same size and same shape, and that one of them is cut by some plane. The intersection is an ellipse, and as the "diameter" of this ellipse we take $x = \sqrt{(\xi_1 \xi_2)}$, where ξ_1 and ξ_2 are the major and minor axes of the ellipse. If the major and minor axes of the elliptical section through the centre of the body are $\sigma_1 \sigma_2$ we similarly define $\rho = \sqrt{(\sigma_1 \sigma_2)}$ as the "diameter" of this section. Then if y is twice the distance of the sectional plane from the centre of the body, and h is the distance between the two tangent planes parallel to the section, we have

$$\frac{y}{h} = \frac{\sqrt{(\rho^2 - x^2)}}{\rho},$$

and hence we can write as before

$$\phi(x) = x \int_0^\infty f(\rho) \frac{d\rho}{\rho \sqrt{(\rho^2 - x^2)}}, \qquad (4.47)$$

where $\phi(x)$ is the probability distribution of the "diameters" of the observed sections and $f(\rho)$ is the probability distribution of the diameters ρ of the central sections of those particles which do intersect the plane, these values ρ being measured in the plane parallel to the section through the centre of the particle. The main problem is to relate $f(\rho)$ to the distribution of the size and shape of the particles. This is difficult since the distribution of ρ is not that of the diameter of the ellipse formed by a random plane through the centre of the particle unless the latter is spherical. This may be best seen by considering ellipsoids which have one axis much longer than the other two, and which are therefore more likely to be intersected by planes perpendicular to the direction of this axis. As a consequence the resulting analysis carried out by Wicksell is rather complicated.

Thin sections

4.19 Krumbein (1935) (Krumbein and Pettijohn, 1938) applied the above theory to the analysis of thin sections of sediments in petrography, assuming the inclusions to be spheres. His original theory neglected the fact that larger spheres have a larger probability of being included in the section. He obtained a closer fit to observed values with the simpler and incorrect theory when examining two samples of sand both by this cross-section method and by actual measurement of the particle size after separation. The reasons for this are not clear and may be connected with the fact that the particles are not in fact spherical. Later work by Greenman (1951a, 1951b), Rosenfeld, Jacobson and Ferm (1953), and Packham (1955), also uses the incorrect equation but obtains good fits to size distribution obtained by sieving.

4.20 If the assumption of sphericity is dropped, we may consider just what can and cannot be deduced by a plane section. Suppose that on the average the number of included bodies in unit volume is λ, that their average volume is v, and that their average surface area is a. Then without further assumptions it does not seem possible to estimate λ. Let λ_p, A_p, and L_p be the average number of intersections with a random plane per unit area, their average area, and their average perimeter, and similarly let λ_l, L_l be the average number of intersections per unit length of a random line, and their average length. These five quantities can be estimated as accurately as we wish by repeated sampling. Clearly,

$$\lambda_p A_p = \lambda_l L_l = \lambda v, \tag{4.48}$$

so that from either plane or line intersection we can estimate the proportion of the volume occupied by particles. $\lambda_p L_p$ will be the average sum of the perimeters of all intersections per unit area, and by (3.3) this will equal $2\pi^{-1}\lambda_l$ multiples of unit length. On the other hand, $4\lambda_l$ units of area will equal the average total surface area of all particles in unit volume by Cauchy's formula derived from (3.52). Thus the total surface area of the particles can be found.

4.21 Although it really belongs to the previous chapter, we may conveniently consider here the problem of the distribution of the intervals formed by the intersection of random lines with convex figures embedded in some volume. We consider only the case where these figures are spherical and such that their diameters have a distribution with the probability density $F(r)$. Let l be the length of an intersection and $g(l)$ the probability distribution of such lengths. The probability of a sphere of radius r intersecting a random line is proportional to $\frac{1}{4}\pi r^2$, and hence if $f_1(r)$ is the probability density of the distribution of r for those spheres which do intersect the line,

$$f_1(r) = \frac{r^2 F(r)}{\int_0^\infty r^2 F(r)\, dr},$$

$$= r^2 F(r)/r_2, \tag{4.49}$$

where r_2 is the second moment about the origin of the distribution of r in a randomly chosen sphere. Let x be the distance of the centre of the sphere from the line. Then the distribution of x, given that an intersection occurs, is

$$8xr^{-2}\, dx \quad (0 \leqslant x \leqslant \tfrac{1}{2}r). \tag{4.50}$$

For a given value of x, the length of the intersection is

$$l = \sqrt{(r^2 - 4x^2)},$$

and hence the distribution of l is

$$2r^{-2}l\, dl \quad (0 \leqslant l \leqslant r). \tag{4.51}$$

The overall distribution of l then has probability density $F(r)$ where

$$g(l) = 2\int_l^\infty lr_2^{-1} F(r)\, dr$$

$$= 2lr_2^{-1}\int_l^\infty F(r)\, dr. \tag{4.52}$$

The solution of this equation is immediately

$$F(r) = \tfrac{1}{2}r_2 \frac{d}{dr}\left\{ \frac{g(r)}{r} \right\}. \tag{4.53}$$

r_2 is probably best obtained by estimating the limit of $2lg(l)^{-1}$ as l tends to zero, since this converges to r_2. As in the previous theory, it is also possible to set up equations connecting the moments of the distribution given by $g(l)$ and that given by $F(r)$. Attempts have been made to generalize (4.52) to cases where the bodies are not spherical, but these do not seem satisfactory.

Figures in three-dimensional space

4.22 Another set of problems closely related to these have been considered, with plane figures and finite linear segments distributed at random in space, and also projections of linear segments on a fixed plane.

Suppose first that circular disks of diameters r are distributed at random in space and are cut by a random plane in intersects of length x. Let $F(r)$ be the probability density of the distribution of the r's, and similarly $\phi(x)$ the probability density of the distribution of the lengths x. The probability that a given disk is cut by the plane is clearly proportional to r, and hence if $f(r)$ is the probability density of the distribution of diameters of the disks which do intersect the plane, we have

$$f(x) = \frac{rF(r)}{\int_0^\infty rF(r)\,dr}$$

$$= r r_0^{-1} F(r),\tag{4.54}$$

where r_0 is the mean diameter of a disk chosen at random. If the plane cuts a disk of diameter r at a distance y from its centre, the distribution of y is $2r^{-1}\,dy$ $(0 \leqslant y \leqslant \frac{1}{2}r)$, and the distribution of x, the length of the intersect, is therefore

$$\frac{x\,dx}{r\sqrt{(r^2 - x^2)}}.$$

We thus obtain

$$\phi(x) = r_0^{-1} \int_x^\infty \frac{xF(r)}{\sqrt{(r^2 - x^2)}}\,dr,\tag{4.55}$$

which is the same equation as (4.37) and may be treated by the same methods.

4.23 Now consider the projections of segments and plane figures. Suppose that linear segments of lengths l are distributed in space with random directions and are such that each length l has a probability distribution with density $F(l)$. Let x be the length of the projection of the segment on a random plane. θ, the angle between the segment and the normal to the plane, will have a distribution $\frac{1}{2}\sin\theta\,d\theta$ $(0 \leqslant \theta \leqslant \pi)$. Given l, the probability distribution of the projection $x = l\sin\theta$ will therefore be

$$xl^{-1}(l^2 - x^2)^{-\frac{1}{2}}\,dx \qquad (0 \leqslant x \leqslant l)$$

and $\phi(x)$, the density of the probability distribution of the projections x, will therefore be given by

$$x^{-1}\phi(x) = \int_x^\infty \frac{F(l)\,dl}{l(l^2 - x^2)^{\frac{1}{2}}}\tag{4.56}$$

This is of the same form as (4.47), the equation used by Krumbein in his approximation. (4.56) can be reduced to an integral equation of Abel's type, and its solution verified to be

$$F(l) = -\frac{2l^2}{\pi}\int_l^\infty \frac{d}{dx}\left(\frac{\phi(x)}{x}\right)\frac{dx}{(x^2 - l^2)^{\frac{1}{2}}}.\tag{4.57}$$

4.24 If we have plane figures of areas a distributed with random orientations in space, and such that a is distributed with probability density $F(a)$, we consider the areas, α say, of their projections on a fixed plane. Suppose that the α's have a distribution with probability density $\phi(\alpha)$. We have $\alpha = a|\cos\theta|$, and $|\cos\theta|$ is uniformly distributed on the range $0 \leqslant |\cos\theta| \leqslant 1$, so that we obtain

$$\phi(\alpha) = \int_\alpha^\infty \frac{F(a)}{a} da \qquad (4.58)$$

whose solution is obviously

$$F(\alpha) = \alpha\phi'(\alpha). \qquad (4.59)$$

Random rotations

4.25 We now consider random rotations in Euclidean space. In two dimensions such a rotation is completely described by an angle through which the body or figure is rotated. The only natural criterion for geometric randomness is the condition that any measurable set of values of θ should have a probability which is invariant under any rotation. It is then obvious that the only probability measure which satisfies this condition is such that the probability of any set of θ's is equal to their Lebesgue measure divided by 2π.

4.26 In three dimensions the situation is much more complicated. We can describe such a rotation either by giving the elements of the orthogonal matrix corresponding to the rotation or by giving the direction cosines (α, β, γ, say) of the axis of rotation, together with the angle (V, say) through which the body is rotated. In either case there are three effectively independent coordinates, and the space of all rotations is three-dimensional.

Once again the natural condition to impose on the probability measure is that it is invariant under any arbitrary rotation. If this is to be true it is natural to assume that these conditions will be satisfied if all directions of the axis of rotation are equally probable (in the sense used in previous chapters) and that the angle of rotation must be uniformly distributed on the range $(0, 2\pi)$. The first of these conclusions is clearly a necessary consequence of the invariance condition, but the second is false. Following Deltheil (1926), we shall now determine the correct distribution of V by using infinitesimal transformations.

4.27 Take rectangular axes of coordinates through the fixed point of the body whose initial position we describe by S_0. We define a "rotation vector" corresponding to the rotation, as a vector whose direction cosines are (α, β, γ)—the direction cosines of the axis of rotation—and whose length is $\tan \frac{1}{2}V$, where V is the angle of rotation. The components of this vector are

$$l = \alpha \tan \tfrac{1}{2}V,$$
$$m = \beta \tan \tfrac{1}{2}V,$$
$$n = \gamma \tan \tfrac{1}{2}V, \tag{4.60}$$

and the elementary probability that we have to find is

$$F(l, m, n)\, dl\, dm\, dn.$$

It is convenient to transform (l, m, n) into homogeneous coordinates which are defined as follows:

$$\lambda = \alpha \sin \tfrac{1}{2}V,$$
$$\mu = \beta \sin \tfrac{1}{2}V,$$
$$\nu = \gamma \sin \tfrac{1}{2}V,$$
$$\rho = \cos \tfrac{1}{2}V. \tag{4.61}$$

Now suppose that the position S_1 is derived from S_0 by the transformation $(\lambda_1, \mu_1, \nu_1, \rho_1)$, the position S_2 from S_1 by $(\lambda_2, \mu_2, \nu_2, \rho_2)$, and S_2 from S_0 by $(\lambda_3, \mu_3, \nu_3, \rho_3)$. Call these rotations R_1, R_2 and R_3 respectively. Our first aim is to express $(\lambda_3, \mu_3, \nu_3, \rho_3)$ in terms of $(\lambda_1, \mu_1, \nu_1, \rho_1)$ and $(\lambda_2, \mu_2, \nu_2, \rho_2)$. To do this we consider first the special case where R_1 and R_2 are rotations through angles π. Such a rotation is known as a "symmetry" (Fig. 4.1).

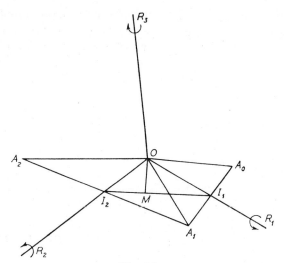

Fig. 4.1

Let (a_1, b_1, c_1) and (a_2, b_2, c_2) be the direction cosines of the axes of R_1 and R_2. The resultant rotation R_3 will have an axis perpendicular to both OR_1 and OR_2. Consider an initial point A_0 which is transformed into A_1 by R_1, and let A_1 be transformed into A_2 by R_2. We can take A_0 in the plane R_1OR_2, and then the total angle through which it is rotated is A_0OA_2, which we denote by V. Then $\frac{1}{2}V =$ angle I_1OI_2, where I_1 and I_2 are the perpendiculars from A_0 and A_1 on the axes OR_1 and OR_2. From the definition above we have

$$\cos \tfrac{1}{2}V = a_1 a_2 + b_1 b_2 + c_1 c_2$$

Since OR_3 is perpendicular to OR_1 and OR_2, its direction cosines are proportional to

$$b_1 c_2 - b_2 c_1,$$
$$c_1 a_2 - c_2 a_1,$$
$$a_1 b_2 - a_2 b_1, \tag{4.62}$$

which are the components of the vector product of OI_2 into OI_1. The magnitude of this vector product is $\sin \frac{1}{2}V$ since $\frac{1}{2}V$ is the angle between OI_1 and OI_2, and hence

$$\lambda_3 = b_1 c_2 - b_2 c_1,$$
$$\mu_3 = c_1 a_2 - c_2 a_1,$$
$$\nu_3 = a_1 b_2 - a_2 b_1, \tag{4.63}$$

and we also have $\qquad \rho_3 = a_1 a_2 + b_1 b_2 + c_1 c_2. \tag{4.64}$

This result holds only for a rotation through an angle π. Now consider a rotation of arbitrary amount. Referring again to Fig. 4.1 and relaxing the condition that A_0 lies in the plane through O perpendicular to OR_3, we see that any rotation about an axis OR_3 can be replaced by the product of two rotations through π about two axes, OS_1 and OS_2 say, perpendicular to OR_3. Moreover, this can be done in an infinity of ways, since we can take for OS_1 any axis perpendicular to OR, OS_2 being then taken at an angle $\frac{1}{2}V$ to OS_1, where V is the required angle of rotation.

Returning to the general case where the rotation $R_3 = (\lambda_3, \mu_3, \nu_3, \rho_3)$ is the result of applying $R_1 = (\lambda_1, \mu_1, \nu_1, \rho_1)$ first and then $R_2 = (\lambda_2, \mu_2, \nu_2, \rho_2)$, we decompose R_1 into two symmetries T_1 and T_1', and similarly R_2 into T_2 and T_2', so that R_3 is the result of applying first T_1, then T_1', then T_2, and finally T_2'. From the arbitrariness of the decomposition of a rotation into symmetries we can choose T_1' and T_2 to be both rotations about the common perpendicular to R_1 and R_2. Their joint effect is therefore to leave the position of the solid unchanged so that R_3 is the result of applying first T_1 and then T_2'.

Let (a_1, b_1, c_1) be the direction cosines of T_1, (a, b, c) those of T_1' and T_2, and (a_2, b_2, c_2) those of T_2'. Then R_1 has the homogeneous coordinates

$$\lambda_1 = b_1 c - b c_1,$$
$$\mu_1 = c_1 a - c a_1,$$
$$\nu_1 = a_1 b - a b_1,$$
$$\rho_1 = a a_1 + b b_1 + c c_1. \tag{4.65}$$

R_2 has the coordinates

$$\lambda_2 = b c_2 - b_2 c,$$
$$\mu_2 = c a_2 - c_2 a,$$
$$\nu_2 = a b_2 - a_2 b,$$
$$\rho_2 = a a_2 + b b_2 + c c_2. \tag{4.66}$$

R_3 has the coordinates

$$\lambda_3 = b_1 c_2 - b_2 c_1,$$
$$\mu_3 = c_1 a_2 - c_2 a_1,$$
$$\nu_3 = a_1 b_2 - a_2 b_1,$$
$$\rho_3 = a_1 a_2 + b_1 b_2 + c_1 c_2, \tag{4.67}$$

and we want to express the latter in terms of the former two. Using (4.65), we solve for (a_1, b_1, c_1) in terms of $(\lambda_1, \mu_1, \nu_1, \rho_1)$ and (a, b, c); and in (4.66) we solve for (a_2, b_2, c_2) in terms of $(\lambda_2, \mu_2, \nu_2, \rho_2)$ and (a, b, c), thus obtaining

$$a_1 = a \rho_1 + b \nu_1 - c \mu_1,$$
$$b_1 = -a \nu_1 + b \rho_1 + c \lambda_1,$$
$$c_1 = a \mu_1 - b \lambda_1 + c \rho_1,$$
$$a_2 = a \rho_2 - b \nu_2 + c \mu_2,$$
$$b_2 = a \nu_2 + b \rho_2 - c \lambda_2,$$
$$c_2 = -a \mu_2 + b \lambda_2 + c \rho_2. \tag{4.68}$$

We also have identically

$$d_1 = a \lambda_1 + b \mu_1 + c \nu_1 = 0,$$
$$d_2 = a \lambda_2 + b \mu_2 + c \nu_2 = 0. \tag{4.69}$$

Inserting (4.68) in (4.67) and using (4.69), we now have

$$\lambda_3 = b_1 c_2 - c_1 b_2 + a_1 d_2 + d_1 a_2,$$
$$= \lambda_2 \rho_1 + \mu_2 \nu_1 - \nu_2 \mu_1 + \rho_2 \lambda_1.$$
$$\mu_3 = c_1 a_2 - a_1 c_2 + b_1 d_2 + d_1 b_2,$$
$$= -\lambda_2 \nu_1 + \mu_2 \rho_1 + \nu_2 \lambda_1 + \rho_2 \mu_1.$$
$$\nu_3 = a_1 b_2 - b_1 a_2 + c_1 d_2 + d_1 c_2,$$
$$= \lambda_2 \mu_1 - \mu_2 \lambda_1 + \nu_2 \rho_1 + \rho_2 \nu_1.$$
$$\rho_3 = a_1 a_2 + b_1 b_2 + c_1 c_2 + d_1 d_2,$$
$$= -\lambda_2 \lambda_1 - \mu_2 \mu_1 - \nu_2 \nu_1 + \rho_2 \rho_1. \tag{4.70}$$

These are the required equations giving the composition of two rotations. We now return to the original coordinates which we take as (l_1, m_1, n_1) for R_1, (l_2, m_2, n_2) for R_2, and (l_3, m_3, n_3) for the resultant of both. We therefore get

$$l_3 = \frac{l_1 + l_2 + m_2 n_1 - m_1 n_2}{1 - l_1 l_2 - m_1 m_2 - n_1 n_2},$$

$$m_3 = \frac{m_1 + m_2 + n_2 \, l_1 - n_1 \, l_2}{1 - l_1 \, l_2 - m_1 \, m_2 - n_1 \, n_2},$$

$$n_3 = \frac{n_1 + n_2 + l_2 \, m_1 - m_2 \, l_1}{1 - l_1 \, l_2 - m_1 \, m_2 - n_1 \, n_2}. \tag{4.71}$$

From this we derive the equations for an infinitesimal transformation by considering the principal parts of $(l_3 - l_2, m_3 - m_2, n_3 - n_2)$ when $l_1 m_1, n_1$ tend to zero. In this way we find, writing (l, m, n) for the common value of (l_2, m_2, n_2) and (l_3, m_3, n_3),

$$\delta l = (1 + l^2) \, l_1 + (lm - n) \, m_1 + (ln + m) \, n_1,$$
$$\delta m = (ml + n) \, l_1 + (1 + m^2) \, m_1 + (mn - l) \, n_1,$$
$$\delta n = (ln - m) \, l_1 + (mn + l) \, m_1 + (1 + n^2) \, n_1,$$

where l_1, m_1, n_1 are small.

We now follow the method of argument used in Chapter 1 and obtain the following equations for the density element $F(l, m, n)$:

$$(1 + l^2) \frac{\partial F}{\partial l} + (lm + n) \frac{\partial F}{\partial m} + (ln - m) \frac{\partial F}{\partial n} + 4lF = 0,$$

$$(lm - n) \frac{\partial F}{\partial l} + (1 + m^2) \frac{\partial F}{\partial m} + (mn + l) \frac{\partial F}{\partial n} + 4mF = 0,$$

$$(ln + m) \frac{\partial F}{\partial l} + (mn - l) \frac{\partial F}{\partial m} + (1 + n^2) \frac{\partial F}{\partial n} + 4nF = 0.$$

Multiplying these by l, $-n$, and m respectively and adding we get

$$(1 + l^2 + m^2 + n^2) \frac{\partial F}{\partial l} + 4lF = 0 \tag{4.72}$$

and there are two similar equations from which we obtain

$$\frac{dF}{F} + \frac{4 \, (l \, dl + m \, dm + n \, dn)}{(1 + l^2 + m^2 + n^2)} = 0, \tag{4.73}$$

and hence F is a multiple of

$$(1 + l^2 + m^2 + n^2)^{-2}. \tag{4.74}$$

We now transform into polar coordinates by the equations

$$l = \tan \tfrac{1}{2} V \sin \theta \cos \phi,$$
$$m = \tan \tfrac{1}{2} V \sin \theta \sin \phi,$$
$$n = \tan \tfrac{1}{2} V \cos \theta. \tag{4.75}$$

Then

$$1 + l^2 + m^2 + n^2 = 1 + \tan^2 \tfrac{1}{2} V = (\cos \tfrac{1}{2} V)^{-2},$$

and

$$dl \, dm \, dn = \tfrac{1}{2} \sin^2 \tfrac{1}{2} V (\cos \tfrac{1}{2} V)^{-4} \sin \theta \, dV \, d\theta \, d\phi$$

so that the element in the parameter space must be

$$dJ = \tfrac{1}{2} \sin^2 \tfrac{1}{2} V \sin \theta \, dV \, d\theta \, d\phi. \tag{4.76}$$

98

The range of variation is $0 \leqslant V \leqslant 2\pi$, $0 \leqslant \theta \leqslant \pi$, $0 \leqslant \phi \leqslant 2\pi$, so that to convert this measure into a probability measure we must multiply by $\frac{1}{2}\pi^{-2}$, obtaining

$$dP = \tfrac{1}{4}\pi^{-2}\sin^2\tfrac{1}{2}V\sin\theta\,dV\,d\theta\,d\phi. \qquad (4.77)$$

Our original guess was that we should choose the axis of rotation at random, and then the angle of rotation uniformly in the range $(0, 2\pi)$. This would give

$$dP = \tfrac{1}{8}\pi^{-2}\sin\theta\,dV\,d\theta\,d\phi,$$

which is therefore wrong.

4.28 The other approach to this problem suggested that an orthogonal transformation be chosen at random by choosing three independent random vectors and orthogonalizing them. Thus we could take a random unit vector $\mathbf{x}_1$ by taking its direction cosines proportional to three independent normal variates. Let $\mathbf{x}_2$ be another such random unit vector, and $\mathbf{y}$ a unit vector parallel to the component of $\mathbf{x}_2$ perpendicular to $\mathbf{x}_1$, which is $\mathbf{x}_2 - \mathbf{x}_1(\mathbf{x}_1.\mathbf{x}_2)$. Then the third vector, $\mathbf{z}$, is defined to be the vector product, $\mathbf{x}_1 \times \mathbf{y}$, and $(\mathbf{x}_1, \mathbf{y}, \mathbf{z})$ can be taken as the unit vectors in a new set of coordinates, and their representation in terms of the unit vectors of the original coordinate system provides the required orthogonal matrix. That this provides the correct orthogonal matrix is nearly obvious, but we shall verify it in detail.

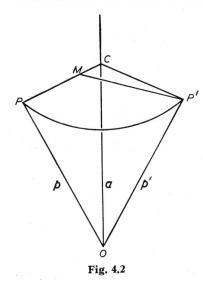

Fig. 4.2

To do this we first consider the representation of the original vector of rotation in terms of an orthogonal matrix by Euler's transformation. Suppose that the rotation was through an angle V about an axis with direction cosines (l, m, n). Let O be the origin of coordinates and $\mathbf{a}$ the unit vector (l, m, n) along the axis of rotation (Fig. 4.2). If P is any point of the body, suppose that it is rotated into a new position P' and that OP, OP' are vectors $\mathbf{p}$ and $\mathbf{p}'$. PC is perpendicular to $\mathbf{a}$, and M is the foot of the perpendicular from P' on PC. Then

$$\mathbf{p}' = \mathbf{OC} + \mathbf{CP}' = \mathbf{OC} + \mathbf{CM} + \mathbf{MP}'.$$

Here

$$OC = (\mathbf{p}.\mathbf{a})\mathbf{a},$$
$$\mathbf{CM} = \mathbf{CP}\cos V$$
$$= (\mathbf{p}-(\mathbf{p}.\mathbf{a})\mathbf{a})\cos V,$$
$$\mathbf{MP'} = (\mathbf{a}\times\mathbf{p})\frac{|\mathbf{CP'}|\sin V}{|\mathbf{p}|\sin\alpha},$$

where α is the angle between OP and OC. Then

$$|\mathbf{CP'}| = |\mathbf{CP}| = |\mathbf{p}|\sin\alpha,$$

so that

$$\mathbf{MP'} = (\mathbf{a}\times\mathbf{p})\sin V.$$

Thus

$$\mathbf{p'} = \mathbf{p}\cos V +(\mathbf{a}\times\mathbf{p})\sin V +(\mathbf{p}.\mathbf{a})\mathbf{a}(1-\cos V),$$

and representing this transformation by a matrix we get

$$\begin{bmatrix} \cos V +l^2(1-\cos V) & lm(1-\cos V)-n\sin V & ln(1-\cos V)+m\sin V \\ lm(1-\cos V)+n\sin V & \cos V +m^2(1-\cos V) & mn(1-\cos V)-l\sin V \\ ln(1-\cos V)-m\sin V & mn(1-\cos V)+l\sin V & \cos V +n^2(1-\cos V) \end{bmatrix}$$

$$(4.78)$$

This gives the matrix representation of the transformation of the coordinates of a point by the given rotation. The effect on the co-ordinate axis would be given by a matrix of the same form with V replaced by $-V$. Notice in particular that the trace of the matrix is $1 +2\cos V$ and depends only on V.

4.29 We now return to the random orthogonal matrix and construct it in a slightly different way. Choose random variables ξ and ϕ which are uniformly distributed on $(-1,1)$ and $(-\pi,\pi)$ respectively, and write for the first row of the matrix

$$\{\xi, \quad (1-\xi^2)^{\frac{1}{2}}\cos\phi, \quad (1-\xi^2)^{\frac{1}{2}}\sin\phi\}. \tag{4.79}$$

These are clearly the coordinates of a unit vector with random direction. Now construct unit vectors $\mathbf{A}$ and $\mathbf{B}$ defined by

$$\mathbf{A} = \{(1-\xi^2)^{\frac{1}{2}}, -\xi\cos\phi, -\xi\sin\phi\},$$
$$\mathbf{B} = \{0, \sin\phi, -\cos\phi\}. \tag{4.80}$$

These are unit vectors which are orthogonal to each other and to the first vector. Write

$$\mathbf{C} = \mathbf{A}\cos\alpha +\mathbf{B}\sin\alpha,$$
$$\mathbf{D} = -\mathbf{A}\sin\alpha +\mathbf{B}\cos\alpha,$$

where α is a random variable uniformly distributed on the interval $(-\pi,\pi)$. Then $\mathbf{C}$ and $\mathbf{D}$ can be taken as the other axes of the new co-ordinate system, and the whole random orthogonal matrix is

$$\begin{bmatrix} \xi & (1-\xi^2)^{\frac{1}{2}}\cos\phi & (1-\xi^2)^{\frac{1}{2}}\sin\phi \\ (1-\xi^2)^{\frac{1}{2}}\cos\alpha & -\xi\cos\phi\cos\alpha+\sin\phi\sin\alpha & -\xi\sin\phi\cos\alpha-\cos\phi\cos\alpha \\ -(1-\xi^2)^{\frac{1}{2}}\sin\alpha & \xi\cos\phi\sin\alpha+\sin\phi\cos\alpha & \xi\sin\phi\sin\alpha-\cos\phi\cos\alpha \end{bmatrix}$$

$$(4.81)$$

which we identify with the matrix previously given. The trace is equal to

$$\xi-\xi\cos\phi\cos\alpha+\sin\phi\sin\alpha+\xi\sin\phi\sin\alpha-\cos\phi\cos\alpha$$
$$=\xi\{1-\cos(\phi+\alpha)\}-\cos(\phi+\alpha). \quad (4.82)$$

The trace, which we identify with $1+2\cos V$, is therefore distributed as

$$\xi(1-\cos\psi)-\cos\psi \quad (4.83)$$

where ξ is uniformly distributed on $(-1,1)$ and ψ is uniformly distributed on $(0,\pi)$. $\cos V$ is therefore distributed as

$$\xi\sin^2\tfrac{1}{2}\psi-\cos^2\tfrac{1}{2}\psi. \quad (4.84)$$

If $w=\cos V$ and we take ψ as fixed, w is distributed uniformly on $(-1,-\cos\psi)$. The probability density of w is therefore proportional to

$$\begin{aligned} f(w)\,dw &= dw\int_{\pi-\cos^{-1}w}^{\pi}(2\sin^2\tfrac{1}{2}\psi)^{-1}\,d\psi \\ &= \tan\tfrac{1}{2}(\cos^{-1}w)\,dw \\ &= 2\sin^2\tfrac{1}{2}V\,dV \end{aligned} \quad (4.85)$$

which agrees with the previous result (4.76) when we insist that positive and negative values of V have equal probabilities. Thus we have proved that the choice of a random rotation is equivalent to choosing a random three-dimensional orthogonal matrix with a probability distribution which is invariant under orthogonal transformations. This distribution is an invariant measure, and since a sample of n quantities from a normal distribution with zero mean can be represented in n-dimensional space by a vector having a distribution which is spherically symmetric, it is natural that these ideas should find application in statistical theory, especially in connection with multivariate analysis. This has been discussed in great detail by James (1954), who applies the theory of invariant measure in the space of all orthogonal $n\times n$ matrices to derive many of the standard distributions used in multivariate analysis.

4.30   It would also be possible to prove an analogue of the "Central Limit Theorem" in the form that the effect of repeated rotations, each specified by a distribution of θ, ϕ, and V, will have a final distribution which should converge to the above one. A sufficient condition for this would probably be that the joint distribution of θ, ϕ, and V must be such that at some point (θ_0, ϕ_0, V_0) there is an open neighbourhood in which the joint probability distribution is differentiable with respect to θ, ϕ, and V.

Application to crystallography

4.31 Another interesting application has been considered by Mackenzie and Thomson (1957) in connection with crystallography. A cube is rotated by a random rotation of the above type and it is desired to find the least angle through which it then needs to be rotated to bring it into the same orientation as before, i.e. having its faces parallel to the faces of its previous position but not necessarily being in the same position. Mackenzie and Thomson studied this problem by Monte Carlo methods, but later Handscomb (1958) and Mackenzie (1958) both obtained the exact distribution.

CHAPTER 5

PROBLEMS OF COVERAGE

Coverage on a plane lattice

5.1 In this chapter we study problems which involve calculating probabilities that certain fixed geometrical figures or sets, usually in the plane, are covered by other figures whose position is in some way random. We begin by considering a particular class of problems which arise when we are given a plane lattice (which need not be rectangular) of points and we wish to study the probability distribution of the number of these points which lie in or on some geometrical figure,such as a circle, whose position in the plane is random. This is the sort of situation which could arise in practice when a circular sampling hoop is thrown at random on to a field in which there are plants whose centres are arranged in a regular lattice.

5.2 The lattice might consist of all points in a plane which have integral coordinates (square lattice), or might consist of the points formed by the vertices of equal equilateral triangles closely packed, or might be of a more general kind. For the most part we consider only the square lattice. If a figure of any fixed shape, and possibly fixed orientation, is thrown at random on to a square lattice, the number of points it covers will be a random variable whose mean will be equal to the measure of the figure if the lattice squares have unit side. This is intuitively obvious but may be proved as in (5.2) below.

Coverage on a line

5.3 The evaluation of the variance is a much more difficult problem even when the figure has a simple shape such as a circle. To illustrate some of the principles involved we begin by considering the much simpler problem of the distribution of the number of lattice points in a random interval placed on a one-dimensional lattice. We suppose the latter to consist of the points $0, \pm 1 \pm 2, \ldots$ and the interval to have length l and random position.

Instead of taking a random interval and fixed lattice we can take a fixed interval and a lattice in random position. Suppose the fixed interval is $(-\tfrac{1}{2}l, \tfrac{1}{2}l)$ and write

$$f(x) = l^{-1} \quad (-\tfrac{1}{2}l \leqslant x \leqslant \tfrac{1}{2}l),$$
$$= 0 \quad \text{elsewhere,}$$

and let the lattice consist of the points T, $T \pm 1$, $T \pm 2$, ..., where T is a random variable uniformly distributed on the interval $(0, 1)$. Then the number of lattice points contained in the interval will be

$$N(T) = l \sum_{n=-\infty}^{\infty} f(T+n), \tag{5.1}$$

whose mean is clearly

$$l \int_{-\infty}^{\infty} f(u)\,du = l. \tag{5.2}$$

The variance of $N(T)$ is

$$l^2 \int_0^1 \sum_{n,s} f(T+n)f(T+s)\,dT - l^2$$

$$= l^2 \sum_{n=-\infty}^{\infty} \int_{-\infty}^{\infty} f(T)f(T+n)\,dT - l^2. \tag{5.3}$$

The integral in (5.3) is equal to

$$l^{-2}(l - |n|) \quad \text{if} \quad |n| \leqslant l \tag{5.4}$$

and is zero otherwise. The variance is therefore

$$\sum (l - |n|) - l^2. \tag{5.5}$$

If $l = p + q$, where p is integral and $0 \leqslant q < 1$, this is equal to

$$q - q^2. \tag{5.6}$$

5.4 We can however look at this problem in another way. The sum for $N(T)$ in (5.1), regarded as a function of T, is periodic with period 1 and can be expanded in a convergent Fourier series

$$N(t) = \sum_{m=-\infty}^{\infty} C_m \exp(-2\pi i m t), \tag{5.7}$$

where

$$C_m = \int_0^1 N(t) \exp(2\pi i m t)\,dt$$

$$= l \int_{-\infty}^{\infty} f(t) \exp(2\pi i m t)\,dt$$

$$= l\sqrt{(2\pi)}\,\phi(2\pi i m), \tag{5.8}$$

where $\phi(u)$ is the Fourier transform

$$\phi(u) = \frac{1}{\sqrt{(2\pi)}} \int_{-\infty}^{\infty} f(t)\,e^{iut}\,dt. \tag{5.9}$$

Parseval's theorem gives

$$\int_0^1 N(t)^2\,dt = \sum_{-\infty}^{\infty} |C_m|^2. \tag{5.10}$$

Since $|C_0|^2 = l^2$ we get

$$\text{var}\,[N(T)] = 2\pi \sum_{-\infty}^{\infty}{}' \,|\phi(2\pi m)|^2, \qquad (5.11)$$

where the sum is taken over all integral values of m except for $m \neq 0$. Inserting the value of $f(t)$, we have

$$\phi(u) = \frac{1}{\sqrt{(2\pi)}} \int_{-\frac{1}{2}l}^{\frac{1}{2}l} l^{-1}\, e^{iut}\, dt$$

$$= \frac{1}{\sqrt{(2\pi)}}\, \frac{\sin \frac{1}{2}lu}{\frac{1}{2}lu} \quad \text{for} \quad u \neq 0,$$

$$= (2\pi)^{-\frac{1}{2}} \quad \text{for} \quad u = 0. \qquad (5.12)$$

Using the above formula, we get

$$\text{var}\,[N(T)] = \frac{2}{l^2\pi^2} \sum_{1}^{\infty} \frac{\sin^2 nl\pi}{n^2}, \qquad (5.13)$$

which is of quite a different form from (5.2) and (5.3). The equality of (5.6) and (5.13) is an example of Poisson's formula (Titchmarsh, 1937, p. 61).

Coverage of a square lattice by a rectangle

5.5 From this it is easy to deduce the result for a rectangle whose position on a lattice is random and whose sides are parallel to the two directions of the lattice, since the number of lattice points covered may be regarded as the product of two independently distributed random variables which are the number of lattice points on a linear lattice covered by random intervals corresponding to the sides of the rectangle. The variance of the number of covered points will vary in a complicated manner. If the sides are l, m, where $l = p+q$, $m = P+Q$ ($0 \leqslant q$, $Q < 1$), the variance is

$$q(1-q)\,Q(1-Q) + l^2\,Q(1-Q) + m^2\,q(1-q). \qquad (5.14)$$

The case where the orientation of the rectangle is also random has not been worked out.

5.6 D. G. Kendall (1948) and R. A. Rankin (Kendall and Rankin, 1953) have considered the similar but more difficult problem of determining the variance of the number of lattice points inside a circle of radius R and random position.

Let the lattice consist of the points (i,j) where $i, j = 0, \pm 1, \pm 2, \ldots$ and write N for the number of these inside the circle $(x-\alpha)^2 + (y-\beta)^2 = R^2$. If $\alpha, \beta = 0$, the determination of N as a function of R is a classical problem in the analytic theory of numbers. It is known that

$$N - \pi R^2 = O(R^{\frac{13}{20}+\varepsilon}) \quad \text{for every } \varepsilon > 0, \qquad (5.15)$$

and Hardy has conjectured that

$$N - \pi R^2 = O(R^{\frac{1}{2}+\varepsilon}) \tag{5.16}$$

for every $\varepsilon > 0$. When the circle is supposed to have a random position the problem becomes simpler in the sense that the mean square of $N - \pi R^2$ can be shown to be $O(R)$. To prove this we have to evaluate the variance of N for fixed R and α, β uniformly and independently distributed on the interval $(0, 1)$. From the above it is clear that $E(N) = \pi R^2$. $E(N^2)$ can be found in two ways.

Let $A(R, \alpha, \beta)$ be the number of lattice points in a circle of radius R with centre (α, β). This is a doubly periodic function in α and β and hence can be expanded, at least formally, in a double Fourier series so that

$$A(R, \alpha, \beta) \sim \sum_{m, n} a_{mn} \exp 2\pi i (m\alpha + n\beta). \tag{5.17}$$

Define $C(n, v)$ to be equal to unity or zero, according as the point (u, v) lies in the circle $u^2 + v^2 \leqslant R^2$ or not. Then

$$A(R, \alpha, \beta) = \sum_{ij} C(i - \alpha, j - \beta),$$

where i, j range over all lattice points. Then

$$
\begin{aligned}
Q_{mn} &= \int_0^1 \int_0^1 A(R, \alpha, \beta) \exp - 2\pi i (m\alpha + n\beta) \, d\alpha \, d\beta \\
&= \sum_{ij} \int_{i-1}^i \int_{j-1}^j C(u, v) e^{2\pi i (mu + nv)} \, du \, dv \\
&= \int \int_{u^2 + v^2 \leqslant R^2} \cos(2\pi mu) \cos(2\pi nu) \, du \, dv \\
&= R(m^2 + n^2)^{-\frac{1}{2}} J_1 \{2\pi R(m^2 + n^2)^{\frac{1}{2}}\}, \tag{5.18}
\end{aligned}
$$

when $m^2 + n^2 > 0$. For $m = n = 0$ we get $Q_{00} = \pi R^2$. We do not need the convergence of the double Fourier series but only the analogue of Parseval's identity which gives

$$
\begin{aligned}
E(N^2) &= \int_0^1 \int_0^1 A(R, \alpha, \beta)^2 \, d\alpha \, d\beta \\
&= \pi^2 R^4 + R^2 \sum \sum {}' (m^2 + n^2)^{-1} J_1^2 \{2\pi R(m^2 + n^2)^{\frac{1}{2}}\}, \tag{5.19}
\end{aligned}
$$

where the double sum $\sum \sum'$ is taken over all values of m and n except $m = n = 0$. Let $r(l)$ be the number of representations of the integer l as the sum of two squares. We can then write

$$E(N^2) = \pi^2 R^4 + R^2 \sum_{l=1}^{\infty} l^{-1} r(l) J_1^2 \{2\pi R l^{\frac{1}{2}}\}. \tag{5.20}$$

These series are convergent because

$$|J_1(z)| < cz^{-\frac{1}{2}}$$

for $z > 0$ and some $c > 0$, and

$$r(l) = O(l^\delta)$$

for every $\delta > 0$. Thus the variance of N is

$$\text{var}(N) = R^2 \sum_{l=1}^{\infty} l^{-1} r(l) J_1^2 \{2\pi R l^{\frac{1}{2}}\}, \qquad (5.21)$$

and using the above bounds we get

$$\text{var}(N) = O(R), \qquad (5.22)$$

so that the standard error of N will increase not faster than $R^{\frac{1}{4}}$, or the square root of the scale factor for the circle. This is in sharp contrast with the case considered before of a random rectangle with sides parallel to the directions of the lattice. Using the asymptotic formula for the Bessel function,

$$J_1(z) \sim \left(\frac{2}{\pi z}\right)^{\frac{1}{2}} \cos\left(z - \tfrac{3}{4}\pi\right)$$

we get

$$\text{var}(N) = R\pi^{-2} \sum_{l=1}^{\infty} l^{-\frac{3}{2}} r(l) \cos^2 [2\pi R l^{\frac{1}{2}} - \tfrac{3}{4}\pi] + o(1). \qquad (5.23)$$

This shows that as $R \to \infty$, $R^{-1}\text{var}(N)$ does not tend to a limit but has upper and lower limits of indetermination which are those of

$$\tfrac{1}{2}\pi^{-2} \sum_{l=1}^{\infty} l^{-\frac{3}{2}} r(l) \{1 - \sin 4\pi R l^{\frac{1}{2}}\}.$$

This in turn certainly lies between zero and

$$a^2 = \tfrac{1}{2}\pi^{-2} \sum_{l=1}^{\infty} l^{-\frac{3}{2}} r(l) = 2\pi^{-2} \zeta\left(\tfrac{3}{2}\right) L\left(\tfrac{3}{2}\right)$$
$$= (0\cdot676497)^2 = 0\cdot457648 \qquad (5.24)$$

Here $\zeta(z)$ is Riemann's zeta function and

$$L(s) = 1^{-s} - 3^{-s} + 5^{-s} - 7^{-s} + \text{etc.}$$

5.7   In the one-dimensional problem we obtained the variance in two different forms and showed that their equality was an example of Poisson's formula. We can do this here also.

Denote by S_N the square whose centre is at the origin and whose sides have lengths equal to $2N + 1$ and are parallel to the axes. This has area $(2N + 1)^2$ and contains $(2N + 1)^2$ points of the lattice. Round each point of the lattice inside S_N we construct a circle of radius R. If two circles have their centres at a distance t apart which is less than $2R$ they will overlap in a region which we may call a "lune" and whose area is easily found to be

$$V(R,t) = 2R^2 \int_0^{\cos^{-1}(t/2R)} \sin^2\theta \, d\theta.$$

$$= R^2 \{\cos^{-1} t (2R)^{-1} - t(2R)^{-1}[1 - t^2(4R^2)^{-1}]^{\frac{1}{2}}\}. \quad (5.25)$$

Let P be a point inside the square S_N and suppose that it is covered by n circles. To each circle we ascribe a density $\frac{1}{2}(n-1)$ at P if P is covered by $n-1$ other circles. If we integrate this density over the whole of the circle, we obtain half the sum of the areas of all lunes formed by this circle and each of the other $(2N+1)^2 - 1$ circles. Thus the total density at P, which is the sum of the densities corresponding to each of the n circles which cover P, is $\frac{1}{2}n(n-1)$, and this is the total number of different lunes formed by pairs chosen out of the $(2N+1)^2$ circles which cover P. Hence the integral of the total density over the square S_N is the sum of the contents of all lunes, or parts of lunes, which are contained in S_N. We denote this by M. Write $p_n(N)$ for the probability that a point chosen at random in the square S_N is covered by n circles. This is equal to the proportion of this square which is covered by n circles. Then

$$M = (2N+1)^2 \sum_{n=0}^{\infty} \frac{1}{2}n(n-1)p_n(N), \quad (5.26)$$

which is, in fact, only a finite series. As $N \to \infty$, $p_n(N)$ will tend to a constant p_n which is the relative fraction of the whole space common to n circles.

5.8 We now find M in a different way. Let $\mathbf{m}$ be a vector from the origin of the lattice to a lattice point and $|\mathbf{m}|$ its length. For fixed R there is only a finite number of different sizes of lune, those for which $0 \leqslant t = |\mathbf{m}| \leqslant 2R$. For $t \geqslant 0$ let $P(t)$ be the number of different $\mathbf{m}$ for which $|\mathbf{m}| = t$. Each circle will contain $P(t)$ lunes corresponding to values of $t \leqslant 2R$, and the total content of all lunes in a circle will be

$$\sum_{0 < t < 2R} P(t) V(R,t) = \sum_{\mathbf{m}}' V(R, |\mathbf{m}|) \quad (5.27)$$

where the second sum is taken over all lattice points except $(0,0)$, and the convention is made that $V(R, |\mathbf{m}|) = 0$ for $|\mathbf{m}| > 2R$. There are $(2N+1)^2$ circles with centres in S_N, and each lune is defined by two of these so that

$$\lim_{N \to \infty} (2N+1)^{-2} M = \frac{1}{2} \sum_{\mathbf{m}}' V(R, |\mathbf{m}|)$$

$$= \sum_{n=0}^{\infty} \frac{1}{2}n(n-1)p_n. \quad (5.28)$$

On the other hand the sum of the areas of all circles or parts of circles inside S_N may be written M', so that

$$R^2 = \lim_{N \to \infty} \frac{M'}{(2N+1)^2}.$$

This must be equal to the integral over S_N of n, the number of spheres covering a point P, and this can be written as

$$\sum_{n=0}^{\infty} np_n = \pi R^2$$
$$= V(R, 0). \tag{5.29}$$

Hence (5.28) can be written

$$\sum_{1}^{\infty} n^2 p_n = \sum_{\mathbf{m}} V(R, |\mathbf{m}|), \tag{5.30}$$

where the sum is now taken over all lattice points including the origin.

Consider a point (α, β), where $(0 \leqslant \alpha \leqslant 1, 0 \leqslant \beta \leqslant 1)$. The number of lattice points contained in a circle with this centre and radius R is equal to the number of circles of radius R and centres on the lattice points, which cover (α, β), i.e. to the value of n for this point. Hence the distribution of the number of lattice points in a random circle of radius R is equal to the distribution of n when (α, β) is chosen at random in the unit square. The variance is therefore

$$\text{var}(N) = \sum_{n=0}^{\infty} n^2 p_n - \left(\sum_{n=0}^{\infty} np_n\right)^2$$
$$= \sum_{\mathbf{m}} V(R, |\mathbf{m}|) - \pi^2 R^4$$
$$= \pi R^2 (1 - \pi R^2) + \sum_{\mathbf{m}}' V(R, |\mathbf{m}|). \tag{5.31}$$

This must also equal (5.5), and so we derive the equation

$$\sum_{l=1}^{\infty} l^{-1} r(l) J_1^2 \{2\pi R l^{\frac{1}{2}}\}$$
$$= \pi (1 - \pi R^2) + \sum_{0 < n \leqslant x} r(n) \{\cos^{-1} n^{\frac{1}{2}} (2R)^{-1} - n^{\frac{1}{2}} (2R)^{-1} [1 - n(4R^2)^{-1}]^{\frac{1}{2}}\}, \tag{5.32}$$

which is a curious and unexpected example of Poisson's formula.

5.9   The oddity about these results is that $\text{var}(N)$ is a sharply oscillating function of R. In practical problems we must therefore calculate it exactly (which is probably best done using the finite series (5.31)), or else use the upper bound Ra^2 given by (5.24)). Some generalizations of these results have been given by Kendall and Rankin to oval curves, to hyperspheres and hyperellipses, and to a hexagonal lattice. The results for oval curves contribute something to our knowledge of the method of "counting squares" in graphical integration, and those for circles thrown on hexagon lattices are useful in the theory of cutaneous sensations. The results are also of some interest in connection with estimating plant numbers in an area by throwing a hoop (or drawing a random circle) in cases where the plants are not distributed in a Poisson field but have a more or less regular pattern.

Random shapes

5.10 In the above problem we have considered the case of a random set (the circle), which has a fixed shape, covering a fixed set (the lattice points). A wide class of problems of a different kind arises when we consider sets which are not only random in position but also in their geometric character. Two examples will illustrate the ideas involved. In the first we consider n intervals of unit length on the line $-\infty < x < \infty$ which are such that their centres x_i are independently distributed with a distribution function $F(x)$. The set of points covered by one or more of these intervals is then a random set.

In the second example we consider n circles of unit radius whose centres fall at random inside a rectangle. The set is defined to consist of all those points inside the rectangle which are covered by one or more circles. In both cases we would like to determine the distribution of the measure of the set.

Robbins' theorem on random sets

5.11 Robbins (1944, 1945) (see also Takacs, 1958) has given a general theorem which makes it possible to obtain the moments. This theorem is contained, in substance, in earlier results of Kolmogoroff (1950) on conditional expectations, but here we follow Robbins' exposition as being more directly relevant to the geometric problem.

We consider Lebesgue measurable sets, X, in an n-dimensional Euclidean space R_n. We suppose that in the space, T, of all such sets there is a probability measure which we denote formally by $\rho(X)$, so that we can write

$$\text{prob}\{X \text{ in } S\} = \int_T C_S(X)\,d\rho(X), \qquad (5.33)$$

where S is a ρ-measurable set of sets X, and $C_S(X)$ is a function of the set X equal to unity if X lies in the set S and equal to zero elsewhere. In all cases we need consider, the set X will be defined by a finite number of parameters, so that T can be taken as a Euclidean space with r, say, parameters $\theta_1, \ldots, \theta_r$. Then the above integral will be a Lebesgue–Stieltjes integral over this space. In the above examples the space T could be taken as defined by the n coordinates of the centres of the intervals in the first case, and the $2n$ coordinates of the centres of the circles in the second case, remembering that there are then $n!$ points in the parameter space which correspond to the same geometrical configuration.

We define a function, $g(x, X)$, of points x in R_n and sets X in T, such that

$$g(x, X) = 1, \quad \text{if } x \text{ belongs to } X,$$
$$= 0, \quad \text{otherwise.} \tag{5.34}$$

Then for fixed X, the Lebesgue integral of $g(x, X)$ over R_n is equal to the Lebesgue measure of X. For fixed x, the probability that x is covered by X will be given by the integral of $g(x, X)$ over the space T. Denote the Lebesgue measure of X by $\mu(X)$, and suppose that $g(x, X)$ is measurable with respect to the product measure in the product space $R_n \times T$. This will be true in all applications. Denote the differential element of the product measure by $d\mu \, \rho(x, X)$. Then, using Fubini's theorem, we have

$$\int_{R_n \times T} g(x, X) \, d\mu \, \rho(x, X) = \int_{R_n} \left\{ \int_T g(x, X) \, d\rho(X) \right\} d\mu(x). \tag{5.35}$$

The inner integral on the right-hand side is the probability that a random set X covers a given point x, which we may write as $P(x \in X)$. Using Fubini's theorem again, we also have

$$\int_{R_n \times T} g(x, X) \, d\mu \, \rho(x, X) = \int_T \left\{ \int_{R_n} g(x, X) \, d\mu(x) \right\} d\rho(X).$$

$$= \int_T \mu(X) \, d\rho(X), \tag{5.36}$$

so that

$$\int_T \mu(X) \, d\rho(X) = \int_{R_n} P(x \in X) \, d\mu(x). \tag{5.37}$$

This means that the expected value of the measure of X is equal to the integral over R_n of the probability $P(x \in X)$. The intuitive idea behind this result is simple. If the space R_n could be divided up into a large number of equal elements so small that each can be regarded as either belonging to X or not, the expected measure of X will be the expected number of these which lie in X multiplied by their common measure. Since the expectation of a sum is equal to the sum of the expectations, even when the variates concerned are dependent, the expected number lying in X will be equal to the sum over all elements of the expectation that each lies in X.

5.12 It is important to extend the above result in such a way that higher moments of $\mu(X)$ can be found. Write $p(x_1, \ldots, x_m)$ for the probability that $x_1, \ldots, x_m$ all belong to X. Then

$$\int_{R_n} p(x_1, \ldots, x_m) \, d\mu(x_1, \ldots, x_m) = \int_T \mu(X)^m \, d\rho(X)$$

$$= E\{\mu(X)^m\}. \tag{5.38}$$

5.13 We can now apply these results to various examples of which the simplest concern random intervals on a line. In the first (Robbins, 1944) we take a fixed interval $(0, 1)$ and N random intervals of length $a < 1$ whose centres are uniformly distributed on the interval $(-\frac{1}{2}a, 1 + \frac{1}{2}a)$. X is defined to be the common part of the interval $(0, 1)$ with the set sum of the N intervals. Then the probability that any point x on $(0, 1)$ is covered by a particular interval is

$$p = \frac{a}{1+a}.$$

If $\mu(X)$ is the measure of X, we then have

$$E\{\mu(X)\} = \int_0^1 p(x)\,dx = \int_0^1 \{1 - (1-p)^N\}\,dx$$
$$= 1 - (1-p)^N. \tag{5.39}$$

In a similar way $E[\mu(X)^2]$ can be found and turns out to be somewhat complicated. A similar problem was considered by Votaw (1946). Here we again have N intervals whose centres are uniformly distributed on an interval, and X is defined to be the set sum of all these intervals. In this case it is possible to find the complete distribution of $\mu(X)$. Votaw also obtains the probability that X contains the whole of the interval. This is a complicated expression which changes its form at a number of points and is very similar to the solution to Stevens' and Fisher's problem (compare (2.38)). In the latter, however, the basic interval on which the centres are distributed is wrapped around a circle, so that we have N random arcs of fixed size, distributed on the circumference of a circle. Robbins' theorem could again be applied to obtain the moments of the part of the circle covered by the arcs.

A problem in virology

5.14 A much more difficult problem, which is due to Professor Fazekas de St. Groth, arises in virology. A virus particle which is taken to be a sphere (whose radius might be 50 $\mu\mu$) is attacked by antibodies which we represent, to a first approximation, as cylinders of length about 37 $\mu\mu$ and effectively negligible thickness. These attach themselves to the virus particles, standing up perpendicularly from the surface. We suppose that N such antibodies are stuck rigidly on the sphere, their points of attachment being distributed independently and at random on the surface. A single such antibody will prevent the virus particle from sticking to a plane surface (in fact a cell) at any point on a circular cap shaded by the antibody. This cap will be a circle whose angular radius is $55°$ and the caps can therefore be regarded as random circles distributed uniformly over the surface of the sphere and possibly overlapping. Given

N (or more generally given the distribution of N), it is required to find the probability that the whole of the surface is shaded.

5.15 No exact solution to this problem is known. If the angular radius of the cap is θ, it is not even known, in general, what is the smallest value of N, as a function of θ, which is such that the sphere can be completely covered (however, this is known for certain particular values of θ). Although it does not seem possible to obtain an analytical expression for the probability that every point of the sphere is covered, it is possible to obtain the first and second moments of the area not covered, both when N is fixed and when it has a probability distribution such as the Poisson.

Suppose the spherical area occupied by the cap is A, where 4π is the whole area of the sphere. Then, using Robbins' theorem, the expected area not covered is

$$4\pi(1 - A(4\pi)^{-1})^N. \qquad (5.40)$$

The second moment can be obtained in the same way, but is more complicated since it is necessary to obtain the probability that two points, separated by an angular distance ϕ, are not covered. This can be found without much difficulty. From the first two moments it is possible, by making certain further assumptions, to find an approximation for the probability that the sphere is completely covered. It is hoped to publish a detailed discussion of this problem at a later date (compare Fazekas and Moran, *Biometrika* (1962), **49**).

5.16 Generalizations of Robbins' results on random intervals have been obtained by Robbins himself (1945), Bronowski and Neyman (1945), Garwood (1947), and Santaló (1947). The first four of these writers consider a fixed rectangle of sides a, b and random parallel rectangles of sides α, β whose centres fall in a rectangle concentric with the fixed rectangle and with sides $a + \alpha$ and $b + \beta$. They obtain the mean and variance of the measure of the set common to the fixed set, and the set-sum of the random intervals. Robbins also obtains the n-dimensional generalization of this, and Santaló considers the case where the random rectangles also have random orientation.

Random circles on a square

5.17 As a further example we consider circles C, falling at random on a square (Garwood, 1947). Suppose that there are N of these, that they have radius a, and that their centres are independently and uniformly distributed over a region T consisting of all points in the plane whose distance from the square, which we call A and take to have unit side, is not greater than a. The area of T is $1 + 4a + \pi a^2$, and the area of each

C is πa^2. The probability of any point of the unit square being covered by at least one circle is clearly

$$1 - \left(\frac{1 + 4a}{1 + 4a + \pi a^2}\right)^N, \tag{5.41}$$

which is therefore equal to the expected area covered. To obtain the second moment consider two points P_1 and P_2 inside A. With a suitable coordinate system these can be represented by (x_1, y_1), (x_2, y_2), where $0 \leqslant x_1, y_1, x_2, y_2 \leqslant 1$. The probability that neither of these points is covered is $q^N(r)$, where $q(r)$ is the fraction of T not inside either of the circles with radius a and centres P_1 and P_2. Since P_1 and P_2 are both inside A, this fraction is a function only of r, the distance between P_1 and P_2. The maximum value of r is $\sqrt{2}$, and if $\phi(r)$ is the probability distribution of r we have

$$E(Y^2) = \int_0^{\sqrt{2}} q^N(r)\phi(r)\,dr. \tag{5.42}$$

Write $\Omega(r)$ for the area common to two circles of radius a whose centres are distant r apart. Then

$$\Omega(r) = 0, \quad \text{if } r \geqslant 2a,$$
$$= 2a^2(\theta - \sin\theta\cos\theta), \quad \text{if } r < 2a, \tag{5.43}$$

where
$$\theta = \cos^{-1} r(2a)^{-1}.$$

Then

$$q(r) = \frac{1 + 4a - \pi a^2 + \Omega(r)}{1 + 4a + \pi a^2}. \tag{5.44}$$

We now have to find $\phi(r)$. We have

$$r^2 = (x_1 - x_2)^2 + (y_1 - y_2)^2.$$

The quantity $\xi = |x_1 - x_2|$ clearly has a distribution with probability density equal to

$$2(1 - \xi)$$

for $0 \leqslant \xi \leqslant 1$, and therefore $u = (x_1 - x_2)^2 = \xi^2$ has the distribution

$$\frac{1 - \sqrt{u}}{\sqrt{u}}\,du. \tag{5.45}$$

$v = (y_1 - y_2)^2$ has the same distribution, and the distribution of $r = \sqrt{(u + v)}$ is found by integrating

$$\frac{(1 - \sqrt{u})(1 - \sqrt{v})}{\sqrt{(uv)}}$$

over the part of the region $r^2 < u + v < (r + dr)^2$ which is contained in the unit square. The probability density is then found to be

G.P.—H

$$\phi(r) = 2r(\pi - 4r + r^2), \quad \text{for } 0 < r < 1,$$
$$= 2r\{4\sin^{-1}r^{-1} + 4\sqrt{(r^2-1)} - r^2 - \pi - 2\}, \quad \text{for } 1 \leqslant r \leqslant 2^{\frac{1}{2}}. \quad (5.46)$$

Inserting (5.44) and (5.46) in (5.42) we obtain $E(Y^2)$ by numerical quadrature.

5.18 In a similar way we can consider circles on a fixed circle. Thus we take a fixed circle A of unit radius and suppose that N random circles of diameters $r\ (r < 1)$ are such that their centres are distributed at random inside a circle concentric with A and having radius $1 + r$. The second moment is then of the form

$$E(Y^2) = \int_0^1 q^N(r)\phi(r)\,dr, \qquad (5.47)$$

where $q(r)$ is given by (5.18) and $\phi(r)$ is the probability density of the distribution of the distance between two points taken at random inside the circle A. This distribution has already been obtained in Chapter 2.

If N were a random variable having some discrete distribution, the first and second moments can be obtained simply by averaging over N. In particular, if N has a Poisson distribution we may imagine circles to be distributed at random on the plane in a Poisson field with some given density. If they touch the area A, their centres must lie in or on the region T and are uniformly distributed over T. This justifies the choice of the particular form of T, quite apart from the fact that it also gives the simplest results.

Robbins (1945) and Garwood (1947) have solved the problem of random circles on a rectangle, and this has been generalized to n dimensions by Santaló (1947).

5.19 A somewhat different class of problems arises when we suppose that the random covering set is not uniformly distributed over some region but has some other distribution. An example of this, discussed by Morgenthaler (1961)—see also Solomon (1958)—is that of a circle of radius R whose centre has a circular bivariate normal distribution about a point O. The random set is defined to be the common part of this circle with a circle of radius r and centre O. If $A(x,y)$ is the overlap of the circles when the first circle has its centre at (x,y) and this point has a circular normal distribution with standard deviation σ, the expected common area is

$$E = (2\pi\sigma^2)^{-1} \int_{-\infty}^{\infty} \int_{-\infty}^{\infty} A(x,y)\exp\left\{-\frac{1}{2\sigma^2}(x^2 + y^2)\right\} dx\,dy. \quad (5.48)$$

Since $A(x,y)$ is a function of $x^2 + y^2$ only, this can be obtained by numerical integration. It can also be expressed in terms of the "offset circular probability function" $p(R,r)$. This is the integral of a circular normal distribution, with unit standard deviation, over a circle of radius R whose centre is distant r from the mean of the distribution. Thus

$$p(R,r) = (2\pi)^{-1} \int\int_{x^2 + y^2 \leqslant R^2} \exp\left[-\tfrac{1}{2}\{(x+a)^2 + (y+b)^2\}\right] dx\,dy,$$

where $a^2 + b^2 = r^2$. We can write this as

$$\frac{1}{2\pi} \int_0^{2\pi} \int_0^R u \exp\left\{-\tfrac{1}{2}(r^2 + u^2 - 2ru\cos\theta)\right\} d\theta$$

$$= \int_0^R u\,e^{-\frac{1}{2}(r^2 + u^2)} I_0(ru)\,du, \tag{5.49}$$

where $I_0(z)$ is the zero order modified Bessel function of the first kind. Using the facts that

$$I_0'(z) = I_1(z),\ I_1(z) + zI_1'(z) = zI_0(z), \tag{5.50}$$

where $I_1(Z)$ is the similar function of the first order, we can transform the above integral into

$$1 - e^{-\frac{1}{2}R^2} - R \int_0^r e^{-\frac{1}{2}(R^2 + u^2)} I_1(Ru)\,du.$$

$$= 1 - q(R,r), \quad \text{say.} \tag{5.51}$$

Tables of $q(R,r)$ have been prepared by the Rand Corporation.

A problem concerning small particles

5.20   A very interesting class of problems of overlap has been considered by Armitage (1949) and Mack (1954). These arise in the counting of dust particles on a sampling plate. The number of these in a given area may be underestimated because of overlapping, and we wish to calculate the expected number of "clumps" of various sizes, a clump being defined as a number of overlapping particles.

The general theory, which we consider first, is due to Mack. We suppose that each particle is represented by a convex figure placed at random on an area A. Let the area a, and perimeter s, of each figure have some given joint distribution, and suppose that the figures are distributed in a Poisson field with density λ. The most convenient way to define the latter condition exactly is to choose some definite point inside each figure which we shall call the "centre", and suppose that these centres are distributed in a Poisson field.

5.21   For simplicity of exposition we consider not a randomly chosen number of figures whose areas and perimeters have a probability distribution, but N figures whose centres are to lie at random in an area A. Of these N figures N_r are to have areas a_r and perimeters s_r ($r = 1, 2,$

$\ldots, k)$, where $N = \Sigma N_r$. We then consider the number of clumps formed by figures whose centres lie in an area α contained in A. The previous problem can then be solved by letting A tend to infinity whilst keeping NA^{-1} fixed and equal to λ.

We define a clump to consist of i figures which overlap, and are not overlapped by any other figure, where $i = 1, 2, \ldots$, so that we include single figures as well. Let C be the expected total number of clumps, and C_i the expected number with i figures. Then

$$\Sigma C_i = C, \tag{5.52}$$

$$\Sigma_i C_i = NA^{-1}. \tag{5.53}$$

We shall prove that for $A\alpha^{-1}$ and N large,

$$C = \alpha A^{-1} \Sigma N_r \exp - \tfrac{1}{2} \Sigma N_u b_{ur}, \tag{5.54}$$

$$C_1 = \alpha A^{-1} \Sigma N_r \exp - \Sigma N_u b_{ur}, \tag{5.55}$$

$$\beta = \alpha \exp - \Sigma N_u a_u A^{-1}, \tag{5.56}$$

where $A b_{ur} = a_n + a_r + s_u s_r (2\pi)^{-1}$, and β is the expected area of α not covered by figures.

The expected number of figures with centres in some small region $\delta\alpha$ of α, which are not covered by other figures, is $p_{11} \delta\alpha$, where p_{11} is the probability that a given figure is not covered by other figures. Since the expectation of a sum is the sum of the expectations, the expected number of single figures in α is $p_{11}\alpha$. We must therefore evaluate p_{11}.

Suppose that the figure is of type i with area a_i and perimeter s_i. Let its function of support, relative to an origin and axis fixed in itself, be $H_i(\theta)$, and suppose that it has orientation ϕ_1. Then its function of support is $H_i(\theta + \phi_1)$, where ϕ_1 can be supposed to be randomly and uniformly distributed on the interval $(0, 2\pi)$. For ϕ_1 fixed, consider the probability that a specified figure of type j, with function of support $H_j(\theta)$ and orientation ϕ_2, does not overlap the first figure. This probability is $1 - A_{ij} A^{-1}$ where A_{ij} is the area of a figure whose function of support is $H_i(\theta + \phi_1) + H_j(\theta + \phi_2)$.

We know that the perimeter and area of a convex figure, with function of support $h(\theta)$, are given by

$$\int_0^{2\pi} h(\theta)\, d\theta$$

and

$$\tfrac{1}{2} \int_0^{2\pi} \{h(\theta)^2 - h'(\theta)^2\}\, d\theta$$

respectively. The expectation of the area A_{ij} is therefore

$$(8\pi^2)^{-1} \int_0^{2\pi} \int_0^{2\pi} \int_0^{2\pi} \{[H_i(\theta + \phi_1) + H_j(\theta + \phi_2)]^2 - [H_i'(\theta + \phi_1) + H_j'(\theta + \phi_2)]^2\}$$
$$d\theta\, d\phi_1\, d\phi_2$$

$$= \tfrac{1}{2} \int_0^{2\pi} \{H_i(\theta)^2 - H_i'(\theta)^2 + H_j(\theta)^2 - H_j'(\theta)^2\}\, d\theta$$

$$+ (2\pi)^{-1} \int_0^{2\pi}\!\!\int_0^{2\pi} H_i(\theta_1) H_j(\theta_2)\, d\theta_1\, d\theta_2$$

$$+ (2\pi)^{-1} \int_0^{2\pi}\!\!\int_0^{2\pi} H_i'(\theta_1) H_j'(\theta_2)\, d\theta_1\, d\theta_2. \tag{5.57}$$

The last term is clearly zero, and so

$$E(A_{ij}) = a_i + a_j + (2\pi)^{-1} s_i s_j.$$

We therefore have

$$C_1 = \alpha A^{-1} \sum_i N_i (1 - b_{ii})^{N_i - 1} \prod_{j \neq i} (1 - b_{ij})^{N_j}, \tag{5.58}$$

and hence (5.55) is true in the limit.

5.22 To calculate C we associate with each clump the point P which is that centre of one of its figures which lies furthest to the right. We can clearly ignore cases where there are two or more such points since their probability is zero. Such a point P is called a right-hand centre. The probability that a right-hand centre falls in a small region of area $\delta\alpha$ will be $p_1 \delta\alpha + o(\delta\alpha^2)$, where p_1 is to be determined. The probability that a right-hand centre P falls in such a region will be the probability that a figure has its centre in this region, and that no other figure overlapping it has a centre further to the right. Let the area to the right of P in which the centres of other figures are not allowed to fall have expectation F_L, and define F_R similarly for left-hand centres. Then $F_L = F_R$ and $F_L + F_R = E(A_{ij})$ so that (5.54) follows. (5.56) can be proved directly from Robbins' theorem.

Armitage (1949) studied this problem in the particular cases where the figures are circles and rectangles and obtained approximate formulae by a quite different method. His results can be derived from Mack's by inserting the particular values of the a_i and s_i.

Lancaster's problem

5.23 A different crowding problem has been considered by Lancaster (1950). Red blood cells in a suspension are counted by spreading a thin film of the blood on a glass slide marked in squares, and counting the number of red cells in each square. If the cells are distributed independently at random the numbers in each square should be distributed in Poisson distributions. This can be tested for by comparing the observed variance of the counts with their mean, since these should be equal for a Poisson distribution. In practice the variance tends to be rather less than the mean, the ratio declining from unity as the mean increases. One cause of this is that cells in the denser squares may tend to be pushed into the less dense squares. Assuming that the cells are smooth circular disks which fall out of the suspension on to the glass slide, we may assume that any cell which arrives unhindered on the slide stays there, but that any cell which falls on top of a cell already on the slide, slides sideways along a radius of the latter until it too lies flat on the glass. Using this model it is possible to calculate the probability that a cell falling out of suspension in a given square is pushed over the boundary into another square, and from this an approximation to the true variance of the number appearing in any square.

5.24 Another class of problems considered by Mack (1948, 1949, 1953)—see also Berg (1945)—is also closely related to the theory of coverage. Suppose that n points are independently distributed at random over a region which may be one-, two- or three-dimensional. A k-aggregate with respect to a figure of defined size, shape, and orientation is defined to be a set of k points which can be covered by such a figure without covering any other point. Mack obtains the expected number of such aggregates in the one-dimensional case where the covering figure is an interval, and in the two-dimensional case where the covering figures are squares, parallelograms, triangles, and circles, and he generalizes some of these results to three dimensions.

5.25 It is evident that further classes of coverage problems can be defined. Mathematically they are not simple and may have to be resolved by sampling experiments. The subject is of relatively recent growth, however, and it appears likely that the emergence of practical problems of the type we have described will give an impetus to considerable further developments.

BIBLIOGRAPHY

APSIMON, H. G. Note 2754. A repeated integral. *Math. Gaz.*, **42** (1958), 52.

ARMITAGE, P. An overlap problem arising in particle counting. *Biometrika*, **36** (1949), 257–266.

BARBIER, E. Note sur le problème de l'aiguille et le jeu du joint couvert. *J. Math. pures et appl.* (2), **5** (1860), 273–286.

BATES, A. E., and PILLOW, M. E. Mean free path of sound in an auditorium. *Proc. Phys. Soc.*, **59** (1947), 535–541.

BATICLE, M. Le problème de la répartition. *Comptes Rendus*, Paris, **196** (1933), 1945–1946; **197** (1933), 632–634; **201** (1935), 862–864.

BERG, W. F. Aggregates in one- and two-dimensional random distributions. *Phil. Mag.* (Series 7), **36** (1945), 337–346.

BERTRAND, J. *Calcul des Probabilités.* Paris (1907).

BITTERLICK, W. Die Winkelzählprobe. *Allg. Forst- u. Holzw. Ztg.*, **59** (1948), 4–5.

BLASCHKE, W. Eine isoperimetrische Eigenschaft des Kreises. *Math. Zeit.*, **1** (1918), 52–57.

BLASCHKE, W. *Vorlesungen über Differential-geometrie. II. Affine Differential-geometrie.* Berlin (1923).

BLASCHKE, W. *Integral-geometrie.* Actualités Scientifiques et Industrielles, No. 252. Hermann et Cie, Paris (1935).

BONDI, H. *Cosmology.* Cambridge (1952).

BONNESEN, T., and FENCHEL, W. Theorie der konvexen Körper. *Ergebnisse der Math.* Springer, Berlin (1934). (Chelsea Reprint, 1948.)

BOREL, E. *Principes et formules classiques du Calcul des Probabilités. Traité du Calcul des Probabilités et de ses Applications.* Paris, Gauthier-Villars (1925).

BRONOWSKI, J., and NEYMAN, J. The variance of the measure of a two-dimensional random set. *Ann. Math. Stat.*, **16** (1945), 330–341.

BUFFON, G. Essai d'arithmétique morale. Supplément à *l'Histoire Naturelle*, Vol. 4 (1777).

BURNSIDE, W. *Theory of Probability* (1928). (Dover reprint, 1959.)

CARTAN, E. Le principe de dualité et certaines intégrales multiples de l'espace tangentiel et de l'espace réglé. *Bull. Soc. Math. France*, **24** (1896), 140–177.

CAUCHY, A. Mémoire sur la rectification des courbes et de la quadrature des surfaces courbes. *Mém. Acad. Sci. Paris*, **22** (1850), 3. (Œuvres complètes (1). Vol. 1 (1908).)

CHALKLEY, H., CORNFIELD, J., and PARK, H. A method for estimating volume–surface ratios. *Science*, **110** (1949), 295–297.

CHANDRASEKHAR, S., and V. NEUMANN, J. The statistics of the gravitational field arising from a random distribution of stars. I. *Astrophys. J.*, **95** (1942), 489–531. II. *Ibid.*, **97** (1943), 1–27.

CHANDRASEKHAR, S. Stochastic Problems in Physics and Astronomy. *Reviews of Modern Physics*, **15** (1943), 1–89.

CHANDRASEKHAR, S. The statistics of the gravitational field arising from a random distribution of stars. III. *Astrophys. J.*, **99** (1944), 25–46. IV. *Ibid.*, **99** (1944), 47–58.

CLARK, A. L. Buffon's Needle Problem. *Canadian J. Research*, **9** (1933), 402 and **11** (1934), 658.

CLARK, P. J., and EVANS, F. C. Distance to nearest neighbour as a measure of spatial relationships in populations. *Ecology*, **35** (1954), 445–453.

CLARK, P. J., and EVANS, F. C. On some aspects of spatial patterns in biological populations. *Science*, **121** (1955), 397–398.

CORNFIELD, J., and CHALKLEY, H. W. A problem in geometric probability. *J. Wash. Acad. Sci.*, **41** (1951), 226–229.

COTTAM, G. A point method for making rapid surveys of woodlands. *Bull. Ecol. Soc. Amer.*, **28** (1947), 60.

COTTAM, G., and CURTIS, J. T. A method for making rapid surveys of woodlands by means of pairs of randomly selected trees. *Ecology*, **30** (1949), 101–104.

COTTAM, G., and CURTIS, J. T. Correction for various exclusion angles in the random pairs method. *Ecology*, **36** (1955), 767.

COTTAM, G., and CURTIS, J. T. The use of distance measures in phytosociological sampling. *Ecology*, **37** (1956), 451–460.

COTTAM, G., CURTIS, J. T., and HALE, B. W. Some sampling characteristics of a population of randomly dispersed individuals. *Ecology*, **34** (1953), 741–757.

COURANT, R., and HILBERT, D. *Methoden der Mathematischen Physik*, I (1931). Springer. (Reprint 1943 by Interscience, New York.)

COX, D. R. Some statistical methods connected with series of events. *J. Roy. Stat. Soc.*, B, **17** (1955), 129–164.

CROFTON, M. W. Sur quelques théorèmes de calcul intégral. *C.R. Acad. Sci. Paris*, **68** (1869), 1469–1470.

CROFTON, M. W. On the theory of local probability, etc. *Phil. Trans.*, **158** (1869), 181–199.

CROFTON, M. W. Geometrical theorems relating to mean values. *Proc. London Math. Soc.*, **8** (1877), 304–309.

CROFTON, M. W. Article "Probability". *Encyclopaedia Britannica*, 9th edn. (1885).

CSASZAR, A. Sur la structure des espaces de probabilité conditionelle. *Acta Math. Acad. Sci. Hung.*, **6** (1955), 337–361.

CZUBER, E. Zur theorie der geometrischen Wahrscheinlichkeiten. *S.-B. Akad. Wiss. Wien*, **90** (1884), 719–742.

CZUBER, E. *Geometrische Wahrscheinlichkeiten und Mittelwerte*. Leipzig (1884).

CZUBER, E. *Wahrscheinlichkeiten und ihre Anwendung auf Fehlerausgleichung, Statistik, und Lebenversicherung*. 2 vols, Leipzig (1908–1910).

DAVIS, H. T. *The Analysis of Economic Time Series*. Principia Press. Bloomington, Indiana (1941).

DELTHEIL, R. Sur la théorie des probabilités géometriques. Thèse. *Annales de la Fac. de Toulouse*, **11** (1919), 1–65.

DELTHEIL, R. *Probabilités Géometriques. Traité du calcul des probabilités et de ses applications*. Gauthier-Villars, Paris (1926).

DOMB, C. The problem of random intervals on a line. *Proc. Cam. Phil. Soc.*, **43** (1947), 329–341.

DOWNTON, F. A note on vacancies on a line. *J. Roy. Stat. Soc.*, B, **23** (1961), 207–214.

DUNN, C. C. Probability method applied to the analysis of recrystallization data. *Phys. Rev.*, (2), **66** (1944), 215–220.

FEJES TOTH, L., and HADWIGER, H. Mittlere Trefferzahlen und geometrische Wahrscheinlichkeiten. *Experientia*, **3** (1947), 366–369.

FELLER, W. *An Introduction to Probability Theory and its Applications*. Wiley, New York (1950).

FISHER, R. A. Tests of significance in harmonic analysis. *Proc. Roy. Soc.*, (A), **125** (1929), 54–59.

FISHER, R. A. On the similarity of the distributions found for the test of significance in harmonic analysis, and in Stevens' problem in geometrical probability. *Ann. Eugenics*, **10** (1940), 14–17.

FRENKEL, J. *Kinetic Theory of Liquids*. Oxford U.P. (1946).

FULLMAN, R. L. Measurement of particle sizes in opaque bodies. *J. Metals*, **5** (1953), 447–452.

FULLMAN, R. L. Measurement of approximately cylindrical particles in opaque samples. *J. Metals*, **5** (1953), 1267–1268.

GARDNER, A. Greenwood's "Problem of Intervals". An exact solution for $n = 3$. *J. Roy. Stat. Soc.*, B, **14** (1952), 135–139.

GARWOOD, F. The variance of the overlap of geometrical figures with reference to a bombing problem. *Biometrika*, **34** (1947), 1–17.

GARWOOD, F. An application of the theory of probability to vehicular-controlled traffic. *J. Roy. Stat. Soc.*, Suppl., **7** (1960), 65–77.

GARWOOD, F., and TANNER, J. C. Note 2800. On note 2754—a repeated integral. *Math. Gaz.*, **52** (1958), 292–293.

GHOSH, B. Random distances within a rectangle, and between two rectangles. *Bull. Calcutta Math. Soc.*, **43** (1951), 17–24.

GILBERT, E. N. Random subdivisions of space into crystals. *Ann. Math. Stat.*, **33** (1962), 958.

GOUDSMIT, S. Random distribution of lines in a plane. *Reviews of Mod. Phys.*, **17** (1945), 321–322.

GREENMAN, N. N. On the bias of grain size measurements made in thin section: a discussion. *J. Geology*, **59** (1951), 268–274.

GREENMAN, N. N. The mechanical analysis of sediments from thin section data. *J. Geology*, **59** (1951), 447–462.

GREENWOOD, M. The statistical study of infectious diseases. *J. Roy. Stat. Soc.*, **109** (1946), 85–103.

GREIG-SMITH, P. *Quantitative Plant Ecology*, Butterworth, London (1957).

GRIDGEMAN, N. T. Geometric probability and the number π. *Scripta Mathematica*, **25** (1960), 183–195.

GROSENBAUGH, L. R. Shortcuts for cruisers and scalers. *Occ. Pap. Sth. For. Exper. Station*, **126** (1952), 1–24.

GROSENBAUGH, L. R. Plotless timber estimates—new, fast, easy. *J. For.*, **50** (1952), 32–37.

GUENTHER, W. C. Circular probability problems. *Amer. Math. Monthly*, **68** (1961), 541–544.

HADWIGER, H. *Altes und Neues über konvexe Körper*. Birkhauser, Basel (1955).

HALL, A. On an experimental determination of π. *Messenger of Math.*, **2** (1873), 113–114.

HALPERIN, M. Some asymptotic results for a coverage problem. *Ann. Math. Stat.*, **31** (1960), 1063–1076.

HAMMERSLEY, J. M. The distribution of distance in a hypersphere. *Ann. Math. Stat.*, **21** (1950), 447–452.

HAMMERSLEY, J. M. A theorem on multiple integrals. *Proc. Camb. Phil. Soc.*, **47** (1951), 274–278.

HAMMERSLEY, J. M. On a certain type of integral associated with circular cylinders. *Proc. Roy. Soc.*, (A), **210** (1951), 98–110.

HAMMERSLEY, J. M. Lagrangian integration coefficients for distance functions taken over right circular cylinders. *J. Math. and Phys.*, **31** (1952), 139–150.

HAMMERSLEY, J. M. Note 2936. On note 2871. *Math. Gazette*, **44** (1960), 287–288.

HAMMERSLEY, J. M., and MORTON, K. W. A new Monte Carlo technique: antithetic variates. *Proc. Camb. Phil. Soc.*, **52** (1956), 449–475.

HANDSCOMB, D. C. On the random disorientation of two cubes. *Canadian J. Math.*, **10** (1958), 85–88.

HARTMAN, P., and WINTNER, A. On the needle problem of Laplace and its generalisations. *Bol. Mat.*, **14** (1941), 260–263.

HERTZ, P. Über die gegenseitigen Durchschnittlichen Abstand von Punkten, die mit bekannter mittlerer Dichte im Raum angeordnet sind. *Math. Ann.*, **67** (1909), 387–398.

HILDEBRAND, J. H. The liquid state. *Proc. Phys. Soc.*, **56** (1944), 221–239.

HILDEBRAND, J. H., and MORRELL, M. E. The distribution of molecules in a model liquid. *J. Chem. Phys.*, **4** (1936), 224.

HOLTSMARK, W. Über die Verbreiterung von Spektrallinien. *Phys. Zeit.*, **20** (1919), 162–168; 25 (1924), 73-84.

HORÁLEK, V. A contribution to the study of the structure of materials. (Czech.) *Aplik. Mat.*, **3** (1958), 376–383.

HOSTINSKY, B. A new solution of Buffon's needle problem. (Czech.) *Rospravy České Akademie*, Classe II, **26** (1917).

HOSTINSKY, B. Sur une nouvelle solution du problème de l'aiguille. *Bull. Soc. Math.*, 2e série, **44** (1920), 126–136.

HOSTINSKY, B. Sur les probabilités géométriques. *Pub. Fac. Sci. Univ. Masaryk.* Brno (1925).

HOSTINSKY, B. Sur les probabilités relatives à la position d'une sphère à centre fixe. *J. math. pures et appl.*, 9e série, **8** (1929), 35–43.

JAMES, A. T. Normal multivariate analysis and the orthogonal group. *Annals of Math. Stat.*, **25** (1954), 40–75.

KAHAN, B. C. A practical demonstration of a needle experiment to give a number of concurrent estimates of π. *Jour. Roy. Stat. Soc.*, A, **124** (1961), 227–239.

KENDALL, D. G. On the number of lattice points inside a random oval. *Q. J. Math.*, (2), **19** (1948), 1–26.

KENDALL, D. G., and RANKIN, R. A. On the number of points of a given lattice in a random hypersphere. *Q. J. Math.*, (2), **4** (1953), 178–189.

KENDALL, M. G., and STUART, A. *The Advanced Theory of Statistics*, Vols. I and II. London, Charles Griffin (1958, 1961).

KIRKWOOD, J. G., and BOGGS, E. M. The radial distribution function in liquids. *J. Chem. Phys.*, **10** (1942), 394.

KOLMOGOROFF, A. N. Sulla determinazione empirica di una legge di distribuzione. *Giornale dell'Istituto Italiano degli Attuari*, **4** (1933), 83–91.

KOLMOGOROFF, A. N. *Foundations of the theory of probability*. Trans. by N. Morrison. Chelsea, New York, 1950.

KRUMBEIN, W. C. Thin section mechanical analysis of indurated sediments. *J. Geology*, **43** (1935), 482–496.

KRUMBEIN, W. C., and PETTIJOHN, F. J. *Manual of Sedimentary Petrography*. New York (1938).

LANCASTER, H. O. Statistical Control in Haematology. *J. Hygiene*, **48** (1950), 402–417.

LAURENT, A. C. Bombing problems. *Operations Research*, **5** (1957), 75–89.

LAZZERINI, M. *Periodico di Mathematica*, **4** (1901), 140.

LEBESGUE, H. Exposition d'un mémoire de Crofton. *Nouvelles Annales de Math.*, (4), **12** (1912), 481–502.

LÉVY, E. B. The point methods of pasture analysis. *New Zealand J. of Agriculture*, **46** (1933).

LÉVY, P. Sur la division d'un segment par les points choisis au hasard. *Comptes Rendus*, Paris, **208** (1939), 147.

LIDWELL, O. M. A simple analysis of the effect of overcrowding on culture plates. *Spec. Rep. Ser. Med. Res. Com.* London, No. 262, 341–342.

LORD, R. D. The distribution of distance in a hypersphere. *Ann. Math. Stat.*, **25** (1954), 794–798.

LYCHE, R. TAMBS. Die Ausdehnung des Schattens, der von einer homogener Kugelschar auf eine Ebene geworfen ist. *Norske Vid. Selsk., Forh.*, **4** (1931), 55–57.

MCCRACKEN, D. D. The Monte Carlo Method. *Scientific American*, **192** (May 1955), 90–96.

MCINTYRE, G. A. Estimation of plant density using line transects. *Ecology*, **41** (1953), 319–330.

MACK, C. An exact formula for $Q_k(n)$, the probable number of k-aggregates in a random distribution of n points. *Phil. Mag.* (Seventh series), **39** (1948), 778–790.

MACK, C. The expected number of aggregates in a random distribution of points. *Proc. Cam. Phil. Soc.*, **46** (1949), 285–292.

MACK, C. The effect of overlapping in bacterial counts of incubated colonies. *Biometrika*, **40** (1953), 220–222.

MACK, C. The expected number of clumps when convex laminae are placed at random and with random orientation on a plane area. *Proc. Cam. Phil. Soc.*, **50** (1954), 581–585.

MACKENZIE, J. K., and THOMSON, M. J. Some statistics associated with the random disorientation of cubes. *Biometrika*, **44** (1957), 205–210.

MACKENZIE, J. K. Second paper on statistics associated with the random disorientation of cubes. *Biometrika*, **45** (1958), 229–240.

MACKENZIE, J. K. Sequential filling of a line by intervals placed at random and its application to linear adsorption. *J. Chemical Physics*, **37** (1962), 723.

MANTEL, L. An extension of the Buffon needle problem. *Ann. Math. Stat.*, **22** (1951), 314–315; **24** (1953), 674–677.

MAULDON, J. G. Random division of an interval. *Proc. Camb. Phil. Soc.*, **47** (1951), 331–336.

MINKOWSKI, H. Volumen und Oberfläche. *Math. Ann.*, **57** (1903), 447–495.

MOORE, P. G. Spacing in plant populations. *Ecology*, **35** (1954), 222–227.

MORAN, P. A. P. Measuring the surface area of a convex body. *Ann. of Math.*, **45** (1944), 783–789.

MORAN, P. A. P. The random division of an interval. I. *J. Roy. Stat. Soc.*, Suppl., **9** (1947), 92–98. II. *Ibid.*, B, **13** (1951), 147–150. III. *Ibid.*, B, **15** (1953), 77–80.

MORAN, P. A. P. Numerical integration by systematic sampling. *Proc. Camb. Phil. Soc.*, **46** (1950), 111–115.

MORGENTHALER, G. W. Some circular coverage problems. *Biometrika*, **48** (1961), 313–324.

MORISITA, M. Estimation of population density by spacing method. *Mem. Fac. Sci. Kyushu Univ.*, ser. E, **1** (1954), 187–197.

OBERG, E. N. Approximate formulas for the radii of circles which include a specified fraction of normal bivariate distribution. *Ann. Math. Stat.*, **18** (1947), 442–447.

OLBERS, W. Ueber die Durchsichtigkeit des Weltraums. *Bode's Astronomische Jahrbuch* (1826), 110–121. (Edinburgh, *New Philosophical Journal*, **1** (1826), 141–150.)

PACKHAM, G. H. Volume, weight, and number frequency analysis of sediments from thin section data. *J. Geology*, **63** (1955), 50–58.

PAGE, E. S. The distribution of vacancies on a line. *J. Roy. Stat. Soc.*, (B), **21** (1959), 364–374.

PEPPER, E. D. On density distributions in stellar space. *Proc. London Math. Soc.*, (2), 29 (1929), 98–110.

POINCARÉ, H. *Calcul des Probabilités.* 2nd edn, Paris (1912).

PÓLYA, G. Über geometrische Wahrscheinlichkeiten an konvexen Körpern. *Ber. Verh. sächs. Akad. Leipzig,* 69 (1917), 457–458.

PÓLYA, G. Über geometrische Wahrscheinlichkeiten. *S-B. Akad. Wiss. Wien,* 126 (1917), 319–328.

PÓLYA, G. *Arch. Math. Phys.*, 27 (1918), 135–142.

RADHAKRISHNA RAO, C. On the volume of a prismoid in *n*-space and some problems in continuous probability. *Math. Student,* 10 (1942), 68–74.

RAIMONDI, E. On a problem of geometrical probabilities. *Revista Union Mat. Argentina,* 7 (1941), 106–109.

RAIMONDI, E. On the pairs of secants of a polygon. *Revista Union Mat. Argentina,* 7 (1941), 133–134.

REID, W. P. Distribution of sizes of spheres in a solid from a study of slices of the solid. *J. Math. Phys.*, 34 (1955), 95–102.

RENYI, A. On a new axiomatic theory of probability. *Acta Math. Acad. Sci. Hung.*, 6 (1955), 285–335.

RENYI, A. On a one-dimensional problem concerning random place filling. (In Hungarian.) *Mag. Tud. Akad. Kut. Mat. Intézet Kozlemenyei* (1958), 109–127.

REY PASTOR, J., and SANTALÓ SORS, L. A. *Geometria Integral.* Buenos Aires, 1951.

ROBBINS, H. E. On the measure of a random set. I. *Ann. Math. Stat.*, 15 (1944), 70–74. II. *Ibid.*, 16 (1945), 342–347.

ROBBINS, H. E. Acknowledgement of priority. *Ann. Math. Stat.*, 18 (1947), 297.

ROSENFELD, M. A., JACOBSON, L., and FERM, J. C. A comparison of sieve and thin section technique for size analysis. *J. Geology,* 61 (1953), 114–132.

SANTALÓ, L. A. Sur quelques problèmes de probabilités géométriques. *Tohoku Math. J.*, 47 (1940), 159–171.

SANTALÓ, L. A. Integral geometry 31. On mean values and geometrical probabilities. *Abh. Math. Sem. Hansischen Univ.*, 13 (1940), 284–294.

SANTALÓ, L. A. Generalisation of a problem of geometrical probabilities. *Rev. Union Mat. Argentina,* 7 (1941), 129–132.

SANTALÓ, L. A. The mean value of the number of parts into which a convex domain is divided by *n* arbitrary straight lines. *Rev. Union Mat. Argentina,* 7 (1941), 33–37.

SANTALÓ, L. A. On the probable distribution of corpuscles in a body, derived from their distribution in its cross-sections, and similar problems. *Rev. Union Mat. Argentina,* 9 (1943), 145–164.

SANTALÓ, L. A. Mean value of the number of regions into which a body is divided by *n* arbitrary planes. *Rev. Union Mat. Argentina,* 10 (1945), 101–108.

SANTALÓ, L. A. Las probabilidades geometricas y la geometria integral. *Bol. Fac. Ingeniera Montevideo,* 3, No. 1 (1945), 91–113.

SANTALÓ, L. A. On the length of a space curve as mean value of the length of its orthogonal projections. (In Spanish.) *Math. Notae,* 6 (1946), 158–166.

SANTALÓ, L. A. On the first two moments of the measure of a random set. *Ann. Math. Stat.*, 18 (1947), 37–49.

SANTALÓ, L. A. Probability in geometrical constructions. (In Spanish.) *An. Soc. Ci. Argentina,* 152 (1951), 203–229.

SANTALÓ, L. A. *Introduction to Integral Geometry.* Actualités Scientifiques et Industrielles, No 1198. Hermann, Paris (1953).

SANTALÓ, L. A. Sobre la distribución de los tamaños de corpúsculas contenidos en un cuerpo a partir de la distribución en sus secciones a projecciones. *Trabajos de Estadistica,* 6 (1955), 181–196.

SCHEIL, E. Die Berechnung der Anzahl und Gröszenverteilung kugelformiger Körpern mit Hilfe der durch ebenen Schnitt erhaltenen Schnittkreise. *Zeit. anorg. allgem. Chem.*, 201 (1931), 259–264.

SERRET, I. A. Sur un problème de calcul intégral. *Ann. École norm.*, 6 (1869), 177–185.

SHANKS, R. E. Plotless sampling trials in Appalachian forest types. *Ecology,* 35 (1954), 237–244.

SIBIRANI, F. Alcune probabilità geometriche. *Mem. Accad. Sci. Ist. Bologna Cl. Sci. Fis.*, (10), 1 (1944), 113–123.

SILBERSTEIN, L. Aggregates in random distributions of points. *Phil. Mag.* (Series 7), 36 (1945), 319–336.

SKELLAM, J. G. The mathematical foundations underlying the use of line transects in animal ecology. *Biometrics,* 14 (1958), 385–400.

124

SOLOMON, H. A coverage distribution. *Ann. Math. Stat.*, **21** (1950), 139–140.

SOLOMON, H. Distribution of the measure of a random two-dimensional set. *Ann. Math. Stat.*, **24** (1953), 650–656.

STEINHAUS, H. *Akad. d. wiss. Leipzig, Ber.*, **82** (1930), 120–130.

STEVENS, W. L. Solution to a geometrical problem in probability. *Ann. Eugenics*, **9** (1939), 315–320.

SYLVESTER, J. J. Report of the British Association, **35** (1865), 8–9.

SYLVESTER, J. J. On Buffon's problem of the needle. *Acta Mathematica*, **14** (1891), 185–205.

TAKACS, L. On the probability distribution of the measure of the union of random sets placed in a Euclidean space. *Ann. Univ. Sci. Budapest*, Eotvos Sect. Mat., **1** (1958), 89–95.

THOMPSON, H. R. Distribution of distance to *n*th neighbour in a population of randomly distributed individuals. *Ecology*, **37** (1956), 391–394.

THOMPSON, W. R. General aspects of projectometry. *Biometrika*, **24** (1932), 21–26.

TITCHMARSH, E. C. *Theory of Fourier Integrals.* Oxford (1937).

VARGA, O. Integralgeometrie 3. Croftons Formeln für den Raum. *Math. Zeit.*, **40** (1936), 387–405.

VENTIKOS, G. P. On the mean value of a straight segment in a plane convex region. *Bull. Soc. Math. Grèce*, **22** (1946), 195–197.

VOTAW, D. F. The probability distribution of the measure of a random linear set. *Ann. Math. Stat.*, **17** (1946), 240–244.

WALSH, J. E. Optimum ammunition properties for salvoes. *Operations Research*, **4** (1960), 204–212.

WALTERS, A. G. The distribution of projected areas of fragments. *Proc. Cam. Phil. Soc.*, **43** (1947), 342–347.

WATSON, G. N. *Theory of Bessel Functions.* Cambridge (1944).

WATSON, G. N. Note 2871. A quadruple integral. *Math. Gazette*, **43** (1959), 280–283.

WHITTAKER, E. T., and WATSON, G. N. *A Course of Modern Analysis.* Cambridge (1935).

WHITWORTH, W. A. *Choice and Chance* (1901). Republished by Hafner, New York (1959).

WICKSELL, S. D. The corpuscle problem, Part I. *Biometrika*, **17** (1925), 84–99. Part II. *Ibid.*, **18** (1926), 151–172.

WOLFOWITZ, J. The distribution of plane angles of contact. *Q.J. of Applied Math.*, **7** (1949), 117–120.

ZUBRZYCKI, S. Les inégalités entre les moments des variables aléatoires équivalentes. *Studia Math.*, **14** (1954), 232–242.

INDEX